THE ROMAN MIND AT WORK

PAUL MacKENDRICK

Professor of Classics
University of Wisconsin

AN ANVIL ORIGINAL

under the general editorship of

LOUIS L. SNYDER

ROBERT E. KRIEGER PUBLISHING COMPANY
HUNTINGTON, NEW YORK
1980

To
MY FATHER AND MOTHER
For Great Sacrifice, This Small Return, With Love

Original Edition 1958
Reprint Edition 1980

Printed and Published by
ROBERT E. KRIEGER PUBLISHING COMPANY, INC.
645 NEW YORK AVENUE
HUNTINGTON, NEW YORK 11743

Copyright © 1958 by
Paul MacKendrick
Reprinted by Arrangement with
D. VAN NOSTRAND COMPANY, INC.

Library of Congress Cataloging in Publication Data

MacKendrick, Paul Lachlan, 1914-
    The Roman mind at work.

    Reprint of the edition published by Van Nostrand Rein-
hold Company, New York, which was issued as no. 35 in
series: An Anvil original.
    Bibliography: p.
    Includes index.
    1. Rome—Civilization.   I. Title.
[DG77.M26 1980]   945'.632   80-13022
ISBN 0-89874-200-5

PREFACE

THIS little book had its inspiration in a course in Greek and Roman Culture which Walter R. Agard and I have given together at the University of Wisconsin since 1947. It is planned as a companion volume to his *Greek Mind,* published as an Anvil Book in 1957. Our amicable differences about the importance of Roman culture only increase my admiration of him, which I should like to record with affection here.

Specialists will recognize my debt to predecessors. Those in English are listed in the bibliography; others include Gaetano de Sanctis, for Roman Republican religion; Marcel Durry, on the *Laudatio Turiae;* Matthias Gelzer, on Caesar; Ettore Lepore, on Cicero; and Jean Perret, on Vergil. I am indebted to the Research Committee of the University of Wisconsin Graduate School and to the John Simon Guggenheim Memorial Foundation, for affording me leisure for more monographic studies of which the present book is a by-product; to the American Academy in Rome, for giving me access to books and a pleasant place to work; above all, to my wife, for typing and for support to morale.

Most of the translations are my own. Professor George E. Duckworth checked my translations of the *Stichus* and *Eclogue IV;* for remaining infelicities he is not responsible. For translations reprinted, thanks are due to Messrs. Charles Scribner's Sons, for a passage from Rolfe Humphries' *Aeneid;* B. H. Blackwell, for Professor Havelock's Catullus; Faber and Faber, for Ezra Pound's Propertius; the University of Chicago Press, for Palmer Bovie's *Georgics;* the University of Wisconsin Press, for A. D. Winspear's Lucretius; the Oxford University Press, for M. R. James' *Acts of St. John.* Messrs. Henry Holt, the University of Wisconsin Press, and the *Classical Journal* have generously permitted me to paraphrase here brief excerpts from my previous publications.

Rome   PAUL MACKENDRICK

TABLE OF CONTENTS

PART II—SELECTED READINGS FROM LATIN AND GREEK SOURCES

Part I

THE ROMAN MIND AT WORK

FOREWORD

The conviction behind this book is that the Roman mind is *still* at work, profoundly influencing, in ways we are not always aware of, our politics, our diplomacy, our art and literature, our religious and philosophical attitudes, and our law. The Romans have a double claim upon our attention: as relevant to us, and as important in themselves. The Epilogue discusses their relevance to modern America; here the focus is on the Romans as important in themselves.

Three things tend to conceal that importance from modern students: an all-too-rare, brief, and necessarily elementary exposure to Latin in school; a view of the Romans as soulless imitators of the Greeks; and an over-willingness to accept either the Romans' assessment of themselves as somewhat unattractive Puritans, or Hollywood's picture of them as sadistic, pleasure-mad indulgers in orgies.

First: country-wide, only about seven in every hundred students now have any firsthand acquaintance with the Roman mind at work, and most of these abandon the subject' after two years. Having applied themselves, with more or less devotion and success, to mastering the structure of a sophisticated, complex language, they are then forced by other claims, some legitimate, some not, to stop Latin just at the moment when they might begin to derive both pleasure and profit from going deeper into the intellectual history of a fascinating and important people. Meanwhile, such knowledge of the Romans as most Americans possess is derived second-hand from books like this, which is perhaps better than nothing, but is still a pity.

Second: the Romans suffer from unfair comparisons with the Greeks. The early nineteenth-century Romantic

9

movement exalted things Greek: Phidian sculpture, Peri-
clean democracy, Sophoclean tragedy, Platonic idealism,
and played down the admirably realistic Roman portrait
sculpture, the sturdy middle-of-the-road conservatism of
the Roman Republic at its best, the vitality of Plautine
comedy, the fervid materialism of Lucretian philosophy.
Polemic is pointless; both cultures have virtues—and defects. The important and the honest thing is not to be
blind to either. Roman culture in fact is the result of applying Greek ideals, practically, to Roman life. A third
of the authors quoted in this book wrote Greek. The two
cultures are one; without the Romans as transmitters
we should hardly be aware of our debt to Greece.

Third: the Romans produced a stereotype of themselves
both less attractive and less human than the truth. To find
the Roman behind the propaganda is valuable intellectual
exercise, which an honest Roman republican, who wanted
his portrait bust carved warts and all, would approve.
Romans had human frailties, which it would be dishonest
as well as uninteresting to conceal, but the cinema's version of them as incessantly wallowing in orgies should
not be swallowed whole, either.

Avoiding these three pitfalls, we may perhaps arrive
at an accurate, though necessarily brief and oversimpli-
fied, assessment of the Roman mind.

This book discusses a baker's dozen topics chosen for
the light they cast on the Roman mind. Each is illustrated
by translations, most of them made especially for this book,
from authors ranging in date from mid-Republic to late
Empire. Such a plan necessarily obscures chronology, but
the topics do fall roughly into a time sequence. "Romans
on Their Origins" discusses Rome of the kings (753-509
B.C.). "The Class Struggle" illustrates Roman history
509-264 B.C. The next four sections, on imperialism,
war, creative activity, and the Romans' stereotype of
themselves are best documented from the Republic's
creative period, roughly 264-43 B.C. The next four
sections, on the growth of political corruption, the rise
of the New Conservatism, the manipulation of the state
religion combined with an interest in philosophy, and the
back-to-the-land movement, center chronologically on
the late Republic, 133-31 B.C. The sections on Roman

law, the drift to absolutism, and the progress of Christianity attempt to do justice to some of the intellectual movements of the Empire, from 31 B.C. to A.D. 395.

To derive profit as well as pleasure from studying the life of the mind was a Roman aim. The nature and extent of that profit and pleasure depend finally on the individual reader, but one student's formulation of the results of over thirty years' profitable and pleasurable association with the Roman mind may serve at least as a point of departure for argument. The author finds the Romans *utiles* and *dulces* for six reasons: they are vital, they are complicated, they illustrate the continuity of history, they demonstrate the virtues and vices of a didactic purpose in literature and art, they see a future in tradition, and they point the moral of *noblesse oblige*.

The Romans are vital. This book has been written amid the light, the noise, and the bustle of modern Rome, where at every turn one jostles the living memory of the past. Ancient Romans, with their pride, their flair, their volubility, their love of small children, their political involvement, their business acumen, their love of the land, their penchant for orthodoxy and absolutism, redeemed by frequent rugged individualism, were not very different from their modern counterparts. To recognize this makes ancient history come alive.

The Romans were complicated. To try to understand their history and their character is a constant challenge. The paradoxes of an imperialist republic, of a people who hated kings and yet accepted totalitarianism, who valued law and order, yet practiced violence, are good to bruise the mind on—and they are also the unresolved paradoxes of our own time.

Rome illustrates the continuity of history. Modern Rome's city council meets in a *palazzo* designed by Michelangelo on the footings of an ancient Records Office 2,036 years old. Roman comedy makes a Broadway hit, Roman conservatism supplies tomorrow's political slogans, and Roman religion lies behind the sacrament of the Mass. To recognize such continuity gives perspective and cause for mature reflection on our responsibility to measure up to the best and improve on the worst of the past.

Roman literature and art had a didactic purpose. In an age of intensely personal poetry and fiction, and non-representational art, themselves a legitimate reaction against the deadness of a classicism that followed the letter and not the spirit of antiquity, it may be well to reflect on, and perhaps even occasionally return to, a literature and an art with an unashamed moral purpose.

Romans believed in the future of tradition. Their empire retained republican forms to the end; a poem of A.D. 410 uses the metre and conventions of over four centuries before. Whether the hand of the past is dead or not depends on how the present grasps it. If the contact is firm, and the meeting is between equals, the result, in politics and in aesthetics, can be fruitful.

Romans at their best believed that *noblesse oblige:* that no privilege is deserved unless its holders exercise it with due regard for the rights, and due resolve to improve the lot, of the underprivileged. The Roman ruling class used its privilege irresponsibly and forfeited it to an absolutist régime which forced classes and masses alike to prostrate themselves before it. Our age has seen the dream of a classless society dissolve into the nightmare of a ruthless totalitarian state. Privileged classes still rule the modern world; modern students are among the privileged classes. If the study of the Roman mind at work should prompt any of them to take his responsibilities soberly and conscientiously, this little book will have more than served its purpose.

1

ROMANS ON THEIR ORIGINS

Foundation Legends. One learns much about a people from what they choose to believe about their beginnings, from what they want their origins to have been. Thus, in the teeth of the evidence, Americans cherish legends of universal rustic simplicity and Godfearing austerity among Pilgrims and Puritans, of George Washington refusing to tell a lie. The Romans, too, in the sophisticated days of the late Republic and the early Empire, nurtured tenderly the myths of their origins: Romulus and Remus and the wolf, the Rape of the Sabine Women, and King Tarquin's pride that went before a fall.

The Myth. By the middle of the first century B.C., educated Romans had agreed upon a suitable myth about their beginnings. (*See Readings No. 1a and b.*) According to this myth the Trojan hero Aeneas had come, a refugee, to Italy, expressly to found Rome. The twins Romulus and Remus were his descendants, their mother a Vestal Virgin, their father the god of war; the wicked King Amulius ordered the children abandoned by the Tiber, like Moses in the bulrushes; a shepherd found and reared them. Romulus killed his brother in a quarrel, fortified the Palatine Hill, and ruled alone, advised by a council of a hundred elders. The pioneers in this new outpost, in need of wives, invited their Sabine neighbors to a festival and carried off their daughters. War naturally followed. The maid Tarpeia betrayed the citadel to the Sabines, who by way of reward crushed her to death under their shields. After heroic single combats and divine interventions, the new wives interceded with their fathers for their bridegrooms, and the two peoples settled

13

down in peace. The united people extended their territory by war; at Romulus' death and apotheosis, Rome was supreme in the countryside.

His successors' stories are more briefly told. Numa, a deeply religious man, conversed with nymphs, organized boards of secular priests, fixed the dates of festivals, and dwelt in the Forum in a humble palace, the Regia, piously preserved into historical times and still visible by Vesta's shrine. The epic event of Tullus Hostilius' reign was the successful single combat of Horatius at the bridge against three mighty brothers from Alba Longa. Ancus Martius founded the port of Ostia at the Tiber mouth; in his reign augury flourished—the observation of signs from heaven, —and the Etruscan Tarquin migrated to Rome, pros- pered, gained the throne, carried all before him in war, and built great public works—walls and drains—with forced labor. He was murdered; his successor Servius Tul- lius, early marked for greatness by the miraculous ap- pearance of fire round his head, reorganized the army, completed Tarquin's wall, and united Rome and Latium. His murder stained the beginnings of Tarquin the Proud's ill-omened and tyrannical reign. As in his garden Tar- quin's stick would decapitate the tallest poppies, so from the state he removed upstanding men. With the labor of Roman freemen he built a great temple on the Capitoline in the Etruscan style to Jupiter the Best and Greatest, and, through the Forum, the Cloaca Maxima (Great Drain). At last, his son's rape of the noble Lucretia broke the Roman people's patience; they deposed Tarquin, elected two consuls, and the Roman Republic was born (509 B.C.).

The Archaeological Evidence. This is a tale to stir the blood, as well as to make the flesh creep; naturally, nineteenth-century historians were skeptical of it. More recently, archaeology has confirmed the main outlines of the story. (The inferences and implications are the Ro- mans' own, and not the less fascinating for being biased, anachronistic, or logically unsound.) For example, the Forum cemetery contains burials of the mid-eighth cen- tury B.C.—the traditional date of Rome's founding—and in it inhumation graves of one culture cut into cremation graves of another, which is archaeology's way of confirming the story of the union of Rome with the Sabines. On the Palatine Hill one can see the post-holes of huts belonging to a village contemporary with Romulus' traditional date. Though most of Rome's so-called "Servian" wall is now dated about 378 B.C., some stretches fit traditional dates. On the Capitoline Hill, many feet below the present street level, the foundations are visible of a temple that Tarquin might have built. And a primitive silo on the Palatine, a bit of painted terra-cotta veneer from the Regia, the round, hut-like shape of Vesta's temple, and an ancient cryptic inscription mentioning a king, all add to the objective evidence that monarchical Rome was a historical fact.

Present Projected into Past.   Seven hundred years of manipulation can do remarkable things to historical facts. Cicero, Livy, and their sources, now lost, combine an admirable scepticism *(see Reading No. 1e)* with a natural pride in Rome and an interest in the axes they have to grind. The result is a projection of the present back into the past, which affords an instructive insight into the Roman mind. Thus our extant sources are uninterested in primitive Rome as an unsightly collection of mud huts on a low hill overlooking the Tiber ford, a village untouched by Greek influence or imperialist ambition, with a scratch militia sometimes successful, sometimes not, in guerrilla skirmishes with its neighbors. They persist in seeing Rome as aware from the beginning of her manifest destiny, early evolving that concept of shared citizenship which made of the High Empire one world-wide family all akin to Rome. They can find surprisingly early precedents for the land distribution and planting of colonies with which the nabobs of their own time punished their enemies and rewarded their veterans; for the supremacy of a grave and reverend senate of blue-blooded conservatives, a landed gentry of pedigree and prejudice; for Hellenistic ruler cult; for relations with the Delphic oracle; and for the existence of a formalized, ritualistic state religion which in fact it took the orderly minds of generations of canon lawyers to evolve. And so their picture of early Rome tells us more about them and their age than about the period they purport to describe.

Early Roman History and the Roman Mind.   What

Cicero and Livy wanted their ancestors to have been was a set of stern and upright collection-plate passers and foreclosers of mortgages. So successful has their rhetoric been that this rather forbidding Puritanical picture of the ancient Roman in a stiff white toga, uttering platitudes in stained-glass attitudes, persists to this day to persuade schoolboys of the utter inhumanity of the Roman race, despite evidence to the contrary of the Romans as all too human: passionate, witty, loving children and the Italian land, but capable of violence, cruelty, and lust; a people much more interesting than the stereotype. Though violence is not absent from Livy's pages, the posed picture is in the foreground, with its noble matrons, stiff-lipped heroes, following the stern dictates of social conscience in lives of rustic austerity, vowed to a war to the death against the type of the tyrant whose pride goes before destruction and who tramples civil liberties underfoot. Aristocratic virtue is here, aristocratic initiative and family solidarity, and the belief in the value of discipline and in the didactic function of history. (*See Readings No. 1c and d.*) The tale is told with the persuasive force of the trained rhetorician, and its rigidity is redeemed by Cicero's concept (and coinage) of *humanitas:* the human virtues, especially intelligence and kindliness, which enable us to distinguish our friends from the apes. And behind the façade we can glimpse the real Roman character: skeptical, pessimistic, precise, practical; superstitious, quarrelsome, guileful, bellicose. Above all, to Cicero and Livy this was not *ancient* history. It was immediate and topical. Cicero's spokesman Scipio had been dead 130 years; Tarquin's tyranny had been over for 455; but the passion is Cicero's own, against his contemporary, Caesar, whose creatures had driven him into exile, whose policy daily threatened the aristocratic and intellectual foundations of Cicero's beloved Republic.

2

CLASS STRUGGLE

The "Conflict of the Orders." The Roman ruling class was not undemocratic in theory, only in practice. Therefore, Roman historians, who present in general the ruling-class viewpoint, reproduce such parables as that of the Belly and the Members (*see Reading No. 2a*), whose moral is that plebeians should be satisfied with that station in life to which it has pleased God—or the ruling class—to call them; and write the history of the early Republic as a conflict between patricians and plebeians, in which the plebeians seek, and by a series of secessions or strikes gain, various rights: to assemble, to be protected by their own officers (the tribunes), to intermarry with patricians, and to run for office. But plebeians in power naturally tended to kick away the ladder by which they had climbed, and the result of two hundred years of struggle was a combination of wealthy plebeians with patricians to reserve for themselves political, economic, and social power and prestige. Dynastic intermarriage, bribery at the polls, and sometimes sheer intimidation kept the Republic an oligarchy, which did not always use its wealth and power for the common good, and whose interest in conserving its own stake in the nation was too often so selfish as to brook no rival and no reform. The result, in the first century B.C., was a struggle of nabobs which killed the oligarchy and resulted in one-man imperial rule, at first benevolent, but gradually becoming absolute.

Land Reform. Successful wars expanded Roman territory and increased public lands. In theory, these were to be shared equitably among the soldiers who had fought to win them; in practice, vast tracts were appropriated by the commanding generals. Small farmers, unable to compete with the large plantation-owners, and often absent campaigning for years on end, would mortgage their farms, suffer foreclosure, and drift in desperation to the slums of Rome. Since the Roman army until late in the Republic depended upon a property qualification for recruitment, this trend was self-defeating, and in 133 B.C. a plebeian tribune, Tiberius Gracchus, in part inspired by humanitarian Stoic philosophers, took active steps toward reform. (*See Readings No. 2b and c.*) He proposed to reclaim broad acres from those who held them without title and redistribute them among the poor. Hard feeling among the propertied class resulted in his murder; his brother Gaius continued his policy and came to a similar end. Bitter party strife continued unresolved and hastened the decline and fall of the Roman Republic.

Slavery.   Slaves, usually war captives, complicated the class struggle. Romans in general took slavery for granted, as we do machines; Varro calls them "tools that can talk." Negroes were few; most slaves came from the Greek East and were often better educated than their masters. Slaves numbered 25 per cent to 50 per cent of Rome's population, competed ruinously with free town labor, and generally proved costly and inefficient on the farm. They supplied the gladiatorial schools, where they were trained to fight to the death, enthusiasm for blood sports being a trait which the Romans share with some modern nations. A revolt of gladiators under Spartacus (73-71 B.C.; *see Reading No. 2d*) was cruelly put down, but slavery remained a problem, generally unrecognized, though alleviated somewhat by the kindness of individual masters. (*See Reading No. 2i.*) Slaves might buy their freedom, or be freed by their masters' wills; some freedmen prospered exceedingly (*see Reading No. 2g*); most proved responsible members of a badly needed middle class. Philosophical and Christian notions of human dignity improved the slaves' lot, and the gradual drying-up of the sources of supply reduced their number, but emperors and private citizens still kept huge staffs of slaves as a matter of conspicuous consumption, and the evil did not disappear with the Empire's fall.

Exploiting the Frontier.   One way of closing the

gap between rich and poor, and of removing dissident elements from the centre of things, was to plant colonies to defend the frontier, a practice which in intent and results resembles the exploitation of the American West. In the mid-Republic Rome planted over forty such centers of Romanization in Italy; Gaius Gracchus planned an ambitious program of colonization overseas. When Caesar followed Sallust's advice (*see Reading No. 2e*), and made that program real with some thirty-five colonies in Gaul, Spain, Africa, Greece, and Asia Minor, he provided a place of retirement for his veterans, and a set of concrete symbols of provincial kinship with Rome. Augustus founded over twice as many; some achieved levels of comfort, and perhaps of culture, seldom equalled since in those areas. This wise policy contributed to a provincial renaissance of which the best-known representatives are the Spaniards Seneca, Trajan, and Hadrian, and the African St. Augustine.

Bread and Circuses. With unemployment endemic, and the Italian grain supply inadequate to feed Rome, the state early assumed the responsibility for feeding the population cheaply or (from Gaius Gracchus' time) free. The dole offered opportunity for political manipulation; so did outright gifts of money (*see Reading No. 2f*); there were not lacking those who said that the system demoralized and enslaved the people. Chariot races in the Circus, gladiatorial shows, wild animal fights, and plays were first presented to win votes by candidates for public office, who would later recoup their losses by gouging the provincials. Over chariot-racing (fifty days a year) Romans waxed as enthusiastic as moderns over football. The various racing stables, Greens, Whites, Reds, and Blues, had their avid "fans," and statues were erected to victorious charioteers and race horses. (One emperor allegedly proposed a race horse for the consulship.) Emperors thought these entertainments worth the money if they amused the populace and discouraged it from trouble-making.

Rags to Riches. Early Republican Rome was almost ostentatiously poor: in the mid-third century B.C. it could boast but a single silver service. But, though ploughboys ceased to become president earlier in Roman than in American history, foreign conquest and trade, following the flag, enriched many, and moralizing against excessive luxury begins by 150 B.C. The nabobs of the late Republic possessed fish ponds, art collections, and seaside villas rivaling Hollywood in splendor, and their successors under the Empire rivaled it also in vulgarity. The philosopher Seneca, who extols the simple life, owned six hundred citron-wood tables. Petronius, a satiric novelist of Nero's time (he committed suicide A.D. 66), has immortalized one vulgar parvenu. (*See Reading No. 2g.*) His silver chamber pot, estates where seventy slaves are born in a day, chorus-girl wife, toadying hangers-on, puns, dinner music, and self-praise make George F. Babbitt look like a man of taste and a shrinking violet. The picture is overblown but illuminating, both by contrast with the miserable existence of the poor, and because the study of the foibles of low life often marks a corrupt aristocracy.

Slums and Palaces. Hadrianic Rome (A.D. 117-136) had perhaps a population of a million. Though the Great Fire of 64 had cleaned out the worst slums, too many of the population still lived in tall, rickety firetraps without light, heat, or sanitation. The satirist Juvenal stresses, besides the noise (*see Reading No. 2h*), the ubiquity of Greeks in Rome, the worship of money, the high cost of living, the passion for passive amusement, the mocking of the poor, and the dangers from traffic, footpads, and drunken subalterns. Meanwhile, in the center of Rome rose Nero's Golden House, two hundred acres of private parkland studded with pavilions and palaces (the Coliseum was built over its ornamental pool), and in the countryside rich villas had their summer and winter dining rooms, shaded walks, ball courts, and hot and cold baths. Of course, then as now, the street was the lower-class Roman's living room, and the public baths provided cheap amenities, but the contrast in living conditions remains striking, and darkly presages decline and fall.

Feast and Famine. While Trimalchio's guests fed on their profusion of fantastic dishes, famine might be stalking the neighboring countryside. The provinces were forced to stint themselves to feed Rome, and inefficient land transport left towns away from the sea starving, while seaports were adequately supplied. For half a millennium from Augustus' time (*see Reading No. 2f*) the imperial bureaucracy administered the grain supply; its warehouses and harbor facilities are still to be seen at Ostia, its offices in Trajan's Market in Rome. It maintained a fleet of ships, of from 50 to 1,300 tons burden; shipowners were exempt from local taxes. Its network covered ports and grain-producing areas all over the empire, especially in Sicily, North Africa, and Egypt. Nevertheless, bread riots were common (*see Reading No. 2j*), and philosophers not always handy to catalyze a happy ending. We hear of mobs stoning those suspected of cornering the market, and burning their villas. Forced sale of surpluses and fixed maximum prices were among the emergency measures tried. Inflation complicated matters; in A.D. 301 it cost a laborer a day's pay to buy a peck of wheat.

Public and Private Charity. By the end of the first century A.D. the imperial privy purse had begun to undertake the support of needy Italian children. The interest on loans from the privy purse to farmers in a given area was paid into a special fund for the support of poor boys and girls. Trajan's coins ceaselessly attest this benevolence, which earned for him the title, "Best of Princes." His arch at Beneventum portrays a pair of happy parents carrying their children on their shoulders to meet the Emperor. Hadrian forgave debts to the privy purse, publicly burned the records, and had the ceremony permanently recorded on a marble relief which still survives. The Empress Faustina gave dowries to poor girls. In the late Empire the Theodosian code (*see Reading No. 2k*) attempted to stop the rise of serfdom by assistance to needy parents from imperial funds. The emperors' example provoked a generous competition of private philanthropy in Italy and the provinces. The younger Pliny (about A.D. 61-114) gave 500,000 sesterces to poor boys and girls, and endowed a library in his native town of Como; the Athenian millionaire, Herodes Atticus (A.D. 101-177), shared with the Emperor Hadrian the enormous expense of a new aqueduct for Troy and built for Athens a theater still used for performances of classic drama. Christianity encouraged charity, and it eventually became an official policy of the church hierarchy.

3

MANIFEST DESTINY

Imperialism and the Roman Mind. Americans study Latin today—the few that do—in part because Victorian public schoolboys had studied it. They studied it because they were, many of them, to be proconsuls or subalterns in the Imperial Civil Service, and their masters astutely saw how the lays of ancient Rome could be sung to the tune of "Rule Britannia." Their most articulate product was Rudyard Kipling. Imperialism and colonialism are hate-words nowadays, and, indeed, Roman imperialism at its worst had much that was hateful; at its best it gave to the world it governed a more just, orderly, and efficient government than it had ever known before or was in many areas to know again. This aptitude for ruling subject peoples is an important facet of the Roman mind.

Expansion in Italy. Expelling the Etruscan kings brought upon the young Roman Republic an economic depression to which archaeology testifies. Rome had scarcely rallied when (390 B.C.) she was sacked by the Gauls. But she recovered, built a strong wall, and began to expand in Italy; by 338 she had bested her rivals and neighbors in the Latin League and could proceed to organize Italy. Her methods are fascinating (*see Reading No. 3a*) for their practicality, diversity, ruthlessness, and dawning grasp of the principle that the most stable government rests upon the consent of the governed. The losers' lands came to be distributed in tiny lots among the Roman lower class; in safely subdued cities, conservative and aristocratic local elements were given control, a consistent Roman practice to the end of the Empire. Neighbors who could be depended upon to behave were granted full citizenship, also a continuing policy and a practical one, for it enlisted loyalty to the last. Subversive elements were ruthlessly transplanted, a chapter in the long and bitter history of the world's displaced persons. Navies were confiscated and rival town walls pulled down. Above all, the unity of rivals was undermined; forbidden to intermarry, trade, or deliberate with each other, they were naturally drawn into the orbit of Rome. This policy shows a level of political sagacity and hard common sense far above that of contemporary Greece.

The "Liberation" of Greece. In the third century, Rome's victory over Carthage brought her new provinces and contact with the sophisticated Greeks of Sicily. Search for help against Carthage produced also a Roman alliance with the Greek East (211 b.c.). By 196, Rome, having defeated Philip V of Macedon, found his Greek possessions an embarrassment, since she had not the staff to administer them. Shortage of trained overseas administrators was a constant plague to the Roman, as it is to the American, Republic. Rome apparently had not then any imperialist ambitions in Greece; she had worries elsewhere, and her war-weary troops were eager for demobilization. So, to the astonished delight of the beneficiaries (*see Reading No. 3b*), she proclaimed the "liberation" of Greece. But after Roman troops were evacuated, Greek internal strife and constant appeals to Rome proved unbearably exasperating; by 147, the Senate found it had muddled through to annexation of Macedonia, and the following year a Roman army destroyed historic and prosperous Corinth. Greece had abused her liberty, and Rome, perhaps not without considerations of commercial rivalry, treated her much as she had treated the Latin League two centuries before. In the process, she made contacts with Greek culture which were to affect her own profoundly. (*See Chapter 5.*) From Corinth's fall Roman moralists date the beginning of the influx of luxury and greed into the Republic.

Mare Nostrum. However reluctant the Senate may have been in 196 to assume imperial responsibilities in the East, a generation later the Roman roving ambassador Popillius could issue an ultimatum to a Seleucid king (*see Reading No. 3c*) with all the arrogance of an imperialist at his worst. This conduct reflects a change in personnel rather than in policy. Popillius belonged, not to the former ruling caste, but to an aggressive and high-handed plebeian group with a sorry record for gangster violence. His conduct toward Antiochus almost certainly exceeded his mandate from the Senate. Popillius was the exception that proves the rule. The Mediterranean became a Roman lake—*mare nostrum*—if not in a Roman fit of absence of mind, at least against the Roman people's will. But the Hellenistic monarchies of Alexander the Great's successors, the Antigonids, Seleucids, and Ptolemies, were collapsing one by one. More by accident than by design, Rome happened to be on hand to fill the vacuum and police the world.

In the same year in which Popillius drew his famous circle, a great aristocrat, Aemilius Paulus, triumphed over the King of Macedon. Among the hostages subsequently sent to Rome to guarantee Greek good behavior was Polybius, the future historian of Rome's constitutional strength and stability. (*See Reading No. 8c.*) If he saw Rome's protectorate over Greece as an imperial fulfillment, it was not types like Popillius who brought him to his favorable conclusions about Roman rule.

Rome and the Jews. After King Antiochus of Syria had antagonized the Jews by trying to Hellenize them, they revolted under Judas Maccabaeus, a movement which it was in Rome's interest to foster, as it was in the rebels' interest to flatter Rome. (*See Reading No. 3d.*) The author of *I Maccabees* stresses the economic aspect of Roman imperialism (Spanish mines), Roman ability to inspire terror in recalcitrant princes, but above all, Roman willingness to make alliances. The Senate preferred diplomacy to war, which produced overambitious generals. Stressed also is Roman determination ("patience" in the Authorized Version), the quality which above all made Rome, when she was ready, the mistress of One World.

A century after Maccabaeus, Judea was a Roman protectorate. The Jews helped Caesar against the Pompeians. Jesus was born while his parents were in Bethlehem to register with the Roman tax-collector: "a decree went out from Caesar Augustus that all the world should be taxed."

King Herod, the slaughterer of the innocents, was a
Roman puppet. Roman procurators, not always as well-
intentioned as Pontius Pilate, were appointed by the
Emperor to keep an eye on this trouble spot. Open re-
bellion in A.D. 66 was punished by the destruction of
Jerusalem: a relief on the Arch of Titus in Rome shows
Roman soldiers carrying off the seven-branched candlestick from the Temple. But Roman imperialism was not
in principle anti-Semitic: Jews like St. Paul enjoyed citizenship rights and were exempt from services forbidden
by Jewish Law. Jews even made Roman converts, including, possibly, Nero's beautiful wife Poppaea.

How to Govern a Province. Imperialism implies
provinces; provinces need governors; how did they behave? Not always honorably (*see Chapter 7*), but governors like the Ciceros recognized and lived up to a
high ideal (*see Reading No. 3e*), which alone can make
imperialism tolerable: to provide happiness and security
for the governed. (Especially the wealthy and the conservative; note the solicitude about public debt and subversion.) The governor must, instinctively and because
he actively wants to, *control* himself, his staff, and his
servants. This is the *frein vital,* one of the best and most
neglected of classical ideals. Temptations must be resisted: to appropriate works of art and handsome slaves;
to play favorites, take bribes, practice extortion. The
provincials are Greeks; the recognition of Rome's intellectual debt to them (*see Chapter 5*) is handsome, the
warning against the unscrupulous among them astute.
Cicero even takes into account "public relations," as he
warns irascible Quintus to be tactful and approachable.

In lands war-torn for centuries, cities flowered again,
roads were made safe for travelers, and courts dispensed
real justice. Liberty is lacking, but liberty is incompatible
with empire, and most men value security above it. Yet
the ideal of *humanitas* here is lofty: such administrative
principles as this were evolved by the Roman mind at its
best and held the Empire together for over five centuries.

Velvet Glove and Iron Hand. The Republic's overthrow and the advent of one-man rule meant reorganizing
the provinces. Augustus kept the troublesome ones under
his personal control and left only the peaceful ones to

the Senate. His laureate, Vergil, recognizes (*see Reading No. 3f*) a talent for imperial administration as pre-eminently Roman, and worth more than Greek virtuosity at sculpture, rhetoric, or astronomy. Here is Roman practicality in a nutshell. The instrument of empire is law (*see Chapter 11*); the empire that Rome has won by the arts of war (*see Chapter 4*), she knows how to consolidate by the arts of peace. And that means "to battle down the haughty, to spare the meek." In the name of battling down the haughty, Augustus had warred savagely on far frontiers; his predecessor Caesar had enslaved or killed two-thirds of the population of Gaul. But each was capable, too, of clement, wise imperialism: Caesar gave home rule to municipal towns in Spain; Augustus urbanized Spain and Gaul. Augustus, too, had Horace to remind him, as Kipling reminded Victorians, that imperial sway depends upon a humble and a contrite heart. Augustus delighted to pass as the prince of peace; he dedicated an Altar of Peace in the Field of Mars. Under him an enlarged Civil Service gave the provinces generally honest administration, opened careers to provincials, and gave at least the propertied minority of the Mediterranean world the blessings of the Roman peace.

Under the Empire, as under the Republic, while lower-class provincials often hated their Roman masters, the upper classes usually supported the foreign régime whose law and order guaranteed them prestige and profit. But latent hatreds burst out into revolts like those of A.D. 70 in Gaul and 83-84 in Britain. (*See Readings 3g and h.*) The Gallic revolt was a nationalist movement; it failed because influential Gauls, realizing the practical value of Roman rule, defected. The speech put by Tacitus into the victorious Roman general's mouth presents that gloomy, brilliant, and rhetorical historian at his bitter best. The appeal is to upper-class reason, common sense, and self-interest: "Taxes? You get value for money. Servitude? You get profit and prestige. Wicked Emperors? Harder on Romans than on you, and, like flood or famine, transitory besides. The Roman Empire, too much the darling of fortune, too deep-rooted and disciplined to fall, is your insurance; its fall will involve your own. Revolution means ruin; sell your birthright, and enjoy your mess of pottage." Mixed blessings, and a bitter reading of history, but Tacitus' views of empire are colored by personal grievance: Domitian had blasted his literary career. Other, less biased witnesses give the Empire better marks.

Tacitus' *Agricola*, despite the impassioned rhetoric of its Scottish patriot (*see Reading No. 3h*), is written to glorify a wise Roman governor, Tacitus' father-in-law. There is in its author's heart of hearts a deep admiration for the kind of culture that can produce such a man. Tacitus is a satirist; what evokes satire is the discrepancy between a wicked world and the satirist's ideal. Tacitus' ideal is Roman ways and standards at their, for him, Republican best. Agricola embodies these ideals; Domitian ruined him. So Tacitus' Scottish chief is bitter, and over half rhetorical. Ironically, Domitian's withdrawal of Agricola saved the chieftain's people from further attacks.

"All's Right with the World." Edward Gibbon, the historian of Rome's decline and fall, saluted the Antonine age as the happiest mankind had ever known. An incurably optimistic rhetorician of that age has left us an unbounded panegyric of Roman imperialism (*see Reading No. 3i*), to be used with caution, for no amount of rhetoric can turn the Roman Empire into a democracy, and the orator's own prejudices are those of the pro-Roman privileged minority. But behind the rhetoric lies genuine gratitude for Roman generosity in granting citizenship and self-rule; recognition of Rome's long record of solicitude for what Kipling calls "lesser breeds without the Law"; appreciation of Roman engineering, which made wildernesses fertile, deserts hospitable, and rough places plain. The Romans, on ancient evidence, accomplished more than the ancient equivalent of making the trains run on time. They brought freedom from fear, and such men are no Fascists. Under them at their best Western Europe enjoyed, as never before or since, the blessings of One World. As another panegyricist wrote, in Latin verse hardly better than this translation:

You made one nation out of many races:
And rebels profit from your flag unfurled.
The conquered share your Law's firm basis:
You made one City, where was once a World.

— 4 —

THE ART OF WAR

Murder as a Fine Art? The Romans neither admired nor idealized war; as pragmatists, they learned to live with it. To understand them, we must try to understand how they felt about war. However much we may desire to renounce wars as instruments of national or international policy, wars happen. The Romans faced this fact; honorable men among them sometimes regarded it as a lesser evil. Romans were seldom too proud to fight. They saw this as a wicked and imperfect world, in which reason should but does not prevail. To them, in consequence, war was inevitable, and they preferred winning to losing. Like others, including ourselves, they persuaded themselves that they never made war except to secure peace, and they seldom saw the contradiction in working out as they did a code of conduct for "civilized" warfare. Like others, including the Greeks, they used war as an extension of diplomacy. They thought it worth while to learn to use it efficiently. The results, while often brutal, were significant. We need not admire, nor condone, but an effort to comprehend may make us less naive in the face of some cold hard facts of modern power politics; may even challenge us to find for the world's ills better and more peaceful solutions than the Romans found.

The Rank and File. The reputation of American Marines will help us to understand Roman military tradition. Despite occasional brutality, Marine strength lies in the noncommissioned officers, especially the top sergeants. Generals plan the battles; sergeants and their squads win wars. So it was with Roman centurions. (*See Reading No. 4a.*) From their teens, war was their whole life.

29

First over the wall in a siege here, decorated for bravery in a battle there, they volunteered for service from one end of the Mediterranean to the other. In brief home tours, they bred children for the next generation's army. Scarred and grizzled at fifty, with all their wounds in front, they were ready to serve again as often as they could pass the physical. Ligustinus' speech is rhetorical, of course; the consuls used him to shame the more recalcitrant centurions. We may refuse to admire his pluck; we may damn his judgment. But we must recognize him and his like as instruments of empire. Some veterans, settled on homesteads in the provinces, would marry native women. Their children were citizens; these families indoctrinated barbarians in the Roman way. To them in large part is due the unity of Western culture.

The Sweets of Victory. We can judge a culture by what it makes lists of: for Americans, baseball averages; for ancient Greeks, Olympic victors; for Romans, triumphing generals. For the commanding general and his men who shared the spoils, the triumph (*see Reading No. 4b*) was the reward for hard labor; for the conquered, it was cruel ostentation; for the mob, a spectacular show. Amid the pomp were reminders of mortality: behind the general in his chariot stood a slave to whisper, "Remember you are only human." In a triumph was carried Caesar's laconic despatch, "I came, I saw, I conquered." In a triumph, troops sang marching songs: "Hide your wife; here comes Caesar," or (from about (A.D. 200):

Franks and Bulgars by the thousand at one stroke we slew:
Persians, Persians, Persians, we will do the same to you.

From open temple doors incense was wafted. At the Mamertine Prison, the captives condemned to death were singled out to be strangled. "By Hercules, your bath is cold," said the Numidian prince Jugurtha, as they dropped him into the oubliette after ripping the gold rings out of his ears. From Romulus to Vespasian 320 triumphs are recorded, an average of one every twenty-eight months. Religion, dignity, pride, greed, tragedy: all are here, and all are the stuff of Roman history.

Organization, Discipline, Incentives. The best account of Roman army recruitment, training, and discipline was written by a Greek (*see Reading No. 4c*), himself a general and a diplomat, to demonstrate to his countrymen the futility of resisting Roman arms. Polybius pictures a compulsory service of sturdy and disciplined militia, based on a property qualification and including allied troops. Cavalry and navy are subordinate; cavalry contingents were usually raised outside Italy, and the navy, late in developing, never fought a battle after Actium (31 B.C.). Polybius' appreciation of centurions no doubt derives from his intimacy with an expert, the Roman general Scipio Aemilianus. He salves his Greek pride by reflecting on Roman creative borrowing, a theme to which we shall return. (*See Chapter 5.*) He discusses at length the Roman camp. Roman armies pitched an elaborate one for every night's halt; the generals thought the security was worth the labor. In camp, rotation of guard duty, even the nightly passing of the watchword, was worked out with the infinite capacity for taking pains which marks Roman military genius. So was the system of punishment and rewards. Cudgeling and decimation were cruel but effective; characteristically, the historian passes no value judgment. Pay and allowances were mean; the soldier looked to booty to eke them out. When Marius abolished (about 104 B.C.), the property qualification for army service, he created at one stroke a professional army whose loyalty to its commanders first and its country second produced the sanguinary wars which ruined the Republic.

As Others Saw Them. The army that Polybius praised sacked Carthage (146 B.C.), and Polybius' patron Scipio wept over the ruins, thinking of Troy and vanished empires, and foreseeing the same fate one day for Rome. The reformed Marian army struck terror into Numidians and Teutons. It became an instrument of its successive generals' ambitions, as Romans took Roman lives in six decades of bloody civil war: Sulla against Marius, Pompey against Caesar, Octavian against Antony and Cleopatra. From the wreckage, Augustus, ably seconded by his lieutenant Agrippa, built a permanent standing army, establishing also, with centurions at the core, a personal bodyguard, the Praetorians, who were to figure as king-makers in the later Empire. Meanwhile, in the provinces, the Imperial army guaranteed the Roman peace, policing the frontiers and garrisoning the interior with a total force of some 300,000, half Roman, half native. Josephus, the Jewish historian of Rome's Jewish wars of the middle years of the first century A.D., is obviously (*see Reading No. 4d*) pro-Roman and no Zionist. Yet he gives unequivocal evidence that the Roman army had lost none of its discipline since Polybius' day, 225 years before. All is still precision and regimentation; the troops even cheer by the numbers. And he is aware that the army which, three or four years before he wrote, had destroyed his own people's Holy of Holies is an efficient instrument of empire.

An Emperor's Commendation.   Inscriptions have a way of penetrating into cultural areas which literature never reaches. One such inscription (*see Reading No. 4e*) affords a fascinating insight into the legionary mind at work. In A.D. 128, Hadrian, on an inspection tour of North African garrisons, reviewed the Third Augustan Legion and its auxiliary troops at Lambaesis in Numidia, now French Foreign Legion country, where the Roman camp is especially well preserved. Proud of their emperor's commendation—which to us seems extremely reserved—his troops had his speech carved on marble and set up in front of their headquarters. The inscription has yet another interest: it obviously records the observations of a trained soldier who knows his business, as indeed Hadrian did. The inspection tours in which he spent half his reign were not merely perfunctory; they strengthened forts and tightened discipline by just and rare bestowal of well-earned praise. Yet this same curt soldier was a gifted amateur architect, who built the Pantheon and the great villa at Tivoli; a connoisseur of art whose choice of statues fills modern museums; a romantic whose brooding love for the boy Antinous has inspired a novel; a poet of sorts whose mannered little address to his soul is one of the best known of Roman poems. Here it is, in Byron's translation:

> *Ah! gentle, fleeting,, wav'ring sprite,*
> *Friend and associate of this clay!*

To what unknown region borne
Wilt thou now wing thy distant flight?
No more with wonted humor gay,
But pallid, cheerless, and forlorn.

This complexity, which has caused Hadrian to be saluted as "the first modern man" (no particular compliment), is part, too, of the Roman character, a useful corrective against thinking of Romans as always marching in lock step.

Training Recruits by the Book. As the Roman Empire declined towards its fall, those nostalgic for the good old days thought they saw the predisposing cause in the lax discipline of the army. As early as A.D. 150, we hear of effete Roman soldiers using depilatories, riding on cushions, and keeping watch only over their wine cups. To remind an emperor, perhaps Theodosius I (A.D. 379-395), of what the Roman army had once been like, Vegetius, a Christian and a courtier who never fought a battle, wrote a handbook of military science. (*See Reading No. 4f.*) Its four books are full of curious lore, of which the abridged selection offers only a sample. Also treated in the full work are the use of javelin, bow, and sling; how to rouse a lethargic army to enthusiasm for war games; how to keep troops healthy, quell mutiny, detect readiness for battle, and cope with camels, armored horses, scythe-chariots, and war-elephants. An appendix discusses siegecraft and naval warfare. The book has a cold-blooded quality which is in the Roman military tradition. Late Imperial wars were cold-blooded enough, but Vegetius' wiser precepts (which sound strangely like the most modern analysts of the decline) went unheeded. Shortly after his book was written, the Roman military heritage had passed to the barbarians.

CREATIVE BORROWING

The Roman Attitude toward Literature, Art, and Science. A judicious analyst of the Roman mind will not overemphasize literature as such, nor art for art's sake, nor pure science. The Romans, like modern Americans, were a hard-headed, practical people, to whom poetry, sculpture, and literature were not so much good in themselves as good *for* something. Thus comedy, presented at their own expense by candidates for public office, entertained the plebs and helped to get politicians elected. Love poetry was looked down on: the Latin word for "lyric" means "nonsense." But epic, satiric, and didactic poetry were of some use: they glorified Rome's past, or more or less wholesomely criticized vice, or salutary lessons might be learned from them about atomic physics (*see Reading No. 9f*), farming (*see Reading No. 10f*), or astronomy. History, too, was useful; to point a moral was to adorn a tale (*see Readings No. 2a and 3g*). Cicero's fifty-eight surviving speeches are intensely practical: they bamboozle juries, persuade, exhort, or vilify (*see Reading No. 9g*). Cicero's practical talent for vilification had an ironic result: his fourteen brilliantly caustic speeches against Mark Antony provoked the victim to have the orator murdered. Art, too, was put to practical uses: portrait sculpture memorialized distinguished ancestors; historical reliefs propagandized for the régime. So, too, with science: the Romans did not originate theories, they applied them to problems in architecture and engineering.

The Question of Originality. Nowadays the motto for creative artists tends to be, "Make it new!" A Roman would regard this as at once ridiculous and impossible. A great Roman poet like Vergil consciously aimed at presenting an old thing in a new way, or vice versa. Thus Vergil's great epic, the *Aeneid,* uses the old Homeric meter, the dactylic hexameter; the old decorative epithets and full-dress similes; the old, old story of Troy's fall— all for a new purpose, the glorification of Rome and Augustus, and with a new technique, involving careful working out of intricate patterns, with balanced line-counts based on number mysticism. Or Ovid will do a new thing in an old way, producing a novel versification of the Roman calendar in the old elegiac metre of love poetry, with which, in his *Art of Love* (where every sentence ends with a proposition), he had so scandalized Augustus that he exiled the poet to an obscure port in Rumania. A Roman poet knew and admired the tradition of his craft more than some moderns. Thus, the conventions of comedy were regarded as having been set by the Greek Menander; therefore, the Roman Plautus uses the meters, plots, and type-characters of his Athenian predecessor but naturalizes them into Latin. Roman poets borrowed, but they borrowed creatively, not slavishly, and the result is great art, great not least because it is proudly conscious of its roots in a great tradition. Such creative borrowing has produced much that is admirable in Renaissance and modern poetry, music, the plastic arts, and architecture.

Roman Comedy, at least in Plautus' hands, is un-starched, earthy, broadly farcical, in touch with the people. (*See Reading No. 5a.*) Its conventions include asides, direct addresses to the audience, deliberate violating of dramatic illusion, unabashed announcement by the characters of their own exits and entrances, limitation of the stage-set to the street, where, as we have seen, Mediterranean peoples have their living room. The characters are types derived ultimately from Aristotle's analysis of virtue as lying in a mean between extremes. (*See The Greek Mind, p. 65.*) The extremes are what interest Plautus: misers, misanthropes, strutting generals, parasites, old men with young ideas, clever, stupid, and drunken slaves. A plot often turns on mistaken identity or guileful deception. The plot of the *Stichus* brings two young merchants home

from overseas, loaded with lucre, just in time to prevent
their father-in-law from marrying their wives to other
husbands. This calls for celebration: the focus is on the
slaves, whom Plautus knew well; he is said to have been
one himself. In their bad puns, drinking, dancing, wench-
ing, and cordial relations with their masters, Plautus'
audience could see themselves. Plautus' themes are varied,
his thought simple, his characters Roman, his comic
devices ingenious, his language inventive, his meters as
tricky as Gay or Gilbert. It is all robust, gay, improbable,
amusing, sometimes crude. The later comedy of Terence
is more intellectual; it casts some light on Roman taste
that after Terence Roman comedy never revived.

Alexandrianism.　Roman literature without Greek
influence would have resembled a purely Anglo-Saxon
English literature without contact with the sophisticated
Norman French. Rome's first alliance with the Greek
East (273 B.C.) was made 150 years after the classical
Greek age of Pericles, and a generation after the intellectual centre of Hellenism had shifted from Athens to Alexandria. Romans, consequently, did their creative borrowing from poetry which has a special interest for us, since
Alexandrian poets have qualities like those shown in our
time by Auden, Eliot, and Pound. Specifically, Alexan-
drians like Apollonius, Callimachus, and Theocritus were
intense individualists; their poetry was learned and al-
lusive; finally, within the tradition they were experimentalists. As individualists, they analyzed avidly their own
emotions, especially the passion of love. As learned men,
they wrote for their fellow intellectuals, who could appreciate the evocative force of allusion in poetry, and not for
the man in the street. As experimentalists, they exploited
unhackneyed myths, injected rationalism into their religious poetry, and wrote pattern poems, with carefully
balanced groups of lines converging upon a core of meaning: poems constructed like a nest of boxes which one
takes apart one after another until the precious inmost
one is reached. The Romans, ever ready, as Polybius re-
marks in another context (*see Reading No. 4c*), to appreciate and use the best work of other peoples, creatively
borrowed from this poetry, as Elizabethans in England
borrowed from Renaissance Latin. Among the most gifted

Roman heirs of Alexandria were Catullus, Vergil, and Propertius.

Roman Lyric is represented here (*see Reading No. 5b*) by Catullus' letter to a friend who had lent his house for the poet's clandestine meetings with his lovely, passionate, fickle, and sophisticated mistress, whom he has immortalized as Lesbia. The poem tells by indirection the poet's whole tragic life story: the bitter-sweetness of lost love remembered, the fruitless journey East to forget, the visit there, at Troy, to the grave of a brother untimely dead, the infatuated attempt to gloss over Lesbia's infidelities, the wistful contemplation of his friend's happiness in a requited, married love which the poet can never enjoy, and his unshakable faith in an unworthy woman. The poem's tone is such that we are not surprised to learn that shortly after writing it Catullus died, burnt out at thirty. A romantic, even a mawkish, story; but the mawkishness is redeemed by the poet's imposing upon his emotion the intellectual control of perfect form. The essence of what is miscalled "classical restraint" lies in this controlled excitement. The poem's core, the inmost and most precious of the boxes, is the poet's sorrow for his brother. The core is enclosed four times over, with its themes arranged A-B-C-D; core; D-C-B-A: Allius—Lesbia—Laodamia————Troy—the brother's death—Troy—Paris—Lesbia—Allius. The two myths, of Laodamia and Paris, are chosen for their double reference to Troy and to the poet's love. Such perfection of form, anticipating the exquisite music of Bach and Mozart, gives keen intellectual pleasure.

Pastoral and Epic. The young Vergil borrows creatively from Catullus. Vergil's *Fourth Eclogue* (*see Reading No. 5c*) is full of reminiscences of the older poet. Perfection of form is there, too: the scheme is 3-7-7-28-7-7-4; the first and last of seven sections total seven lines; the core contains four times seven, and the paired sections which enclose it have seven lines each. The poet hymns, like Isaiah, the birth of a child, perhaps Octavian's. The theme throughout is newness of life: a new baby, a new peace, a new addition (in the forty-ninth line, seven times seven) to the roster of the gods, a new poetry. The Eclogue is one of ten, all arranged in a

pattern unified in form and content. They foreshadow the
maturity which produced Rome's greatest epic, the
Aeneid, also carefully patterned. Its hero, Aeneas, is a
refugee, a bearer of burdens, a man capable of self-de-
nial for a higher goal (he leaves Dido, who loves him,
to found a new nation in Italy), a man who has known
Hell, and is acquainted with grief and with battles and
the untimely death of friends. In his heroic aspect, Aeneas
is the ideal Roman, for whom *noblesse oblige*—perhaps
an idealized portrait of Octavian-Augustus. In his humanity, his power of sympathy, he reflects Vergil's own
sensitive spirit. And finally, holding as he does a child
by the hand, his burden his father and his gods, a city
in flames behind him, he is universal history; he is ourselves.

Love Poetry enjoyed a brief Indian summer in
Augustan Rome. Its great names are Horace, witty and
untranslatable; Tibullus, charming but anaemic; Ovid,
clever, salacious, facile; and the neurotic and tortured
Propertius, presented here (*see Reading No. 5d*) in an
equally neurotic and tortured modern poet's translation,
inaccurate in the letter, perfect in the spirit, of the
original. The original is interesting less for its structure—
three simple ten-line sections—than as illustrating the
conventions of the *genre,* wherewith the poet binds himself hand and foot, then dances as though free. In conven-
tional Latin love elegy the *bacillus amatorius'* incubation
period is as short as in a Hollywood film. The victim
cannot sleep; he bristles with Cupid's darts like a pin-
cushion. His mistress, whose promises are written in running water, would as soon scratch his eyes out as look at
him, or sooner. He promises her poetic immortality; she
prefers cash down. He therefore sighs for the primitive
past, when men were so happy and so poor. Her faithlessness throws him into a decline. Perhaps he will die; if
so, will she have the following epitaph inscribed on his
tombstone? Our Propertian sample is typical: the midnight summons, the interior monologue, the anticipated
recriminations, the commonplace that all the world loves
a lover, the death wish. What seems to matter is elegance,
but behind the elegance is a tortured spirit.

A Silver Age of Roman literature followed the

Golden Age of Augustus. Decline is implied, and decadence is real. Epigrams hurtle like shuttlecocks; the
style of a Silver Age author like Seneca (*see Reading
No. 2i*) reminded Macaulay of a constant diet of anchovy
sauce. Form is exalted over matter, rhetoric becomes an
end instead of a means. Roman rhetoric, borrowed, rather
uncreatively, from Greek, is impressive in structure. It
divides the art of persuasion into show speeches, speeches
of advice, and courtroom speeches. It categorizes figures
of speech and thought. It analyzes the processes of invention, composition, choice of style (florid, medium, or
severe), memorizing, and delivery. It prescribes six parts
for a speech: prologue, statement of case, statement of
subdivisions, proof, refutation, and tailpiece, in which
last the orator goes up into the air like a Roman candle,
followed, he hopes, by his audience's delirious enthusiasm.
Such schematization is overrigid; it produced orators for
an age when orators were muzzled.

The great Silver Age figure is Tacitus. His speeches
(*see Readings No. 3g and h*) use such rhetorical devices
as paradox, antithesis, simile, metaphor, commonplace,
and exaggeration, and one speech contradicts another.
But Tacitus is master, not servant, of his rhetoric, which
faithfully reflects his own schizophrenia. He sighs for a
dead past which he knows he overidealizes, which cannot
return, and, if it did, would be ephemeral.

Roman Portraits are the glory of Roman art, to
which we now turn from literature. The best of them
date from the late Republic, and show that practicality
which we have emphasized as so thoroughly Roman. For
they were derived from the masks of ancestors, as carried
in Roman funeral processions, and their function was
to glorify the past of aristocratic clans, to immortalize
the hard-faced men who made the Roman Empire. The
faces that stare us down in the museums are unidealized;
the sculptor, following orders, reproduced his subject as
he was, warts and all, with his wrinkles, his beak of a
nose, his battle scars. Creative borrowing is there, too,
from such fine Hellenistic heads as that of Euthydemus
of Bactria in the Torlonia Museum in Rome. After 150
years of forced adulation of bad Roman copies of Greek
originals, critics are rediscovering and genuinely admiring

Roman portrait sculpture. Augustus' Altar of Peace, vowed in 13 B.C., uses Greek techniques for a practical Roman purpose, to exalt the Prince of Peace and his lieutenants, who appear in relief on the monument, along with a grave, bearded Aeneas and allegorical figures. Later in the Empire, Trajan's column, more a document than a work of art, unrolls in a great scroll of over twenty-five hundred figures the deeds of Trajan and his army in the conquest of Dacia.

Roman Architecture shows Roman practicality at its creative best. Already in the Republic, Roman architects were using a new and enormously strong material—concrete—for magnificent, axially symmetrical structures with arch and vault like the Sanctuary of Fortune at Praeneste, the ancestor of the more grandiose complexes of the Empire. These also took advantage of the freedom which poured concrete gives the architect, to enclose space in any shape he likes, without confining himself to the rectangular. Hadrian's buildings—the Pantheon, the Temple of Venus and Rome, the enormous Villa—show soaring architectural imagination; the great Baths in Rome survive to testify to the might and majesty of the later Empire. Uncreative borrowing in the Renaissance and after has put Roman architecture out of fashion, but its techniques are still useful. The Romans also exploited, if they did not invent, city planning: plans like Bernini's for the Square of St. Peter's in Rome, or L'Enfant's for Washington, D. C., are ultimately Roman in origin. And Roman roads, bridges, and aqueducts gave the Mediterranean world an ease of communication and a level of sanitation not reached again till the nineteenth century.

— 6 —

THE ROMAN CHARACTER

Great Men and Roman History. The concrete Roman mind would be impatient of modern studies of historical trends. To a Roman, great men—and great women—made history. So Roman historians will, not without rhetorical flourishes and unfair comparisons, highlight strong personalities. A poet will immortalize old-fashioned austerity, a bereaved husband will eulogize a heroic wife, a nephew write an admiring memoir on a pedantic uncle. Too rarely, the makers of history themselves have left, in letters, the plain stamp of their idiosyncrasies. The result is a gallery of portraits whose highlights and chiaroscuro make them vivid and real. They depict a ruling class which bred and sometimes admired self-sacrifice, austerity, hard work, encyclopaedic learning, and fidelity in men and women; rulers whose openhandedness served their ambition or in whom self-deprecation did not preclude firmness. As we have seen before, and will see again, this is not the whole picture, but it is, once more, enough to show how many-faceted was the Roman mind.

Heroes of the Republic, as they appear in Livy's long gallery, and in the sculpture in the Hall of Fame with which Augustus, desiring to link himself with a storied and respectable antiquity, decorated his Forum, express in part Roman patriotism gilding its past, ashamed of its present, and hoping to inspire its future. Not all are stereotypes: consider for example, the proud Coriolanus. When they brought him the decree of banishment for tyrannical conduct, "Banished?" said he with patrician scorn: "*I* banish *you!*" More to the pattern is Cincinnatus,

leaving the plough to assume the dictatorship, returning
to it when the emergency was over; or Decius, sacrificing
himself in the Latin war (*see Reading No. 6a*). His
legendary self-sacrifice became a commonplace, the subject of a drama by Accius, a scupltured relief in the
Forum, and countless references in rhetoric and philosophy. Perhaps most striking to the modern reader in
the story is its formulaic, primitive air. Decius is a scape-
goat, the willing victim of a powerful state religion and
a patrician pontiff. Decius' colleague Torquatus pointed
a stern moral: he executed his own son, for disobeying
orders prohibiting single combat.

The Stiff Upper Lip was prized by the Romans, as it
is by the British, as their most characteristic feature.
Thanks to repeated mention in prose and poetry, the most
famous wearer of this expression was Regulus; the best-
known account, that in a "Roman Ode" of Horace (*see
Reading No. 6b*), here translated in the meter of the
original. Horace, perhaps replying to contemporary
clamor for the release of Roman prisoners in Parthian
hands, portrays Regulus, in magnificent rhetoric, as car-
ing more for Roman honor than for Roman lives, including his own. He is harsh, but no less hard on himself than on the Roman prisoners he advises the Senate
not to ransom. The quiet close, wherein he turns from
wife, family, and friends to go back, keeping his plighted
word, to certain death, is high poetry, in the finest classical tradition both of form and content. The clash of wills
is over, the decision he wanted has been taken, and he is
at peace. To a man like Regulus, his own martydom is
merely an unimportant incident. That the Romans, despite
many lapses, produced many such men is one of their
claims upon our admiration if not upon our affection.

A Puritan. Roman moralists of the Augustan Age
and earlier held up to the admiration of their decadent
contemporaries a foursquare New England Yankee type,
a stern apostle of the religion of "Eat it up, wear it out,
make it do": the elder Cato (*see Reading No. 6c*). The
key to his character, as it is to that of many an ancient
Roman and modern American self-made man, is energy,
combined with versatility and strong conservatism. A
plebeian, without pedigree, he knew and cultivated the

traditional ways to preferment: he learned the law, conducted with great oratorical skill canny prosecutions for
political corruption, and could appeal to a distinguished
career as a soldier. A good hater, he embraced among
his many cordial dislikes Greeks, Carthaginians, and extravagant women. He enjoyed striking a hillbilly pose
among his cultivated fellow senators. A successful capital
farmer (*see Reading No. 10b*), he inveighed against luxury and worked tirelessly for Roman moral, social, and
economic reconstruction, himself setting an example of
rock-like integrity. His stern Puritanism was relieved by a
dry wit: he once remarked that he never made love to his
wife except when there was thunder and lightning, adding
with a twinkle, "I do enjoy a good thunderstorm!"

A Popular Hero. Julius Caesar, whom Sallust
compares with the younger Cato (*see Reading No. 6d*) so
devastatingly to the latter's disadvantage, seems far from
the stereotype of Republican hero; indeed he typifies what
old Cato was afraid would happen to Rome if Greek culture got a foothold. Patrician, cultivated, sensitive, he
was born to lead the aristocrats, but fated to become a
popular hero. His energy and versatility were a match for
old Cato's, but, judging conservatism bankrupt, he used
the popular faction as the tool of his ambition. Sallust
was devoted to him; so were his soldiers and the Roman
mob. Generosity is the keynote of Sallust's hymn of praise
to him, and generosity in politics, generally with other
people's money, is often the mark of the demagogue. But
to Caesar, demagoguery was only a means to an end.
The end was power. In politics and in generalship, power
was what he strove for, with complete mastery of detail.
His every act was part of a calculated whole; he spun no
thread he could not catch up. He was Roman through
and through in his concept of reasonable, calculated, in-
flexible domination, and in his command of the art of
putting the enemy morally in the wrong. He stole the
conservatives' thunder, and they killed him on principle
—which is also an aspect of the Roman way.

A Stoic Saint. Of old Cato's great-grandson, Cicero
wrote, "He thinks he is living in Plato's Republic, and
not among the scum of Romulus." A bronze bust of
him found recently at Volubilis in Morocco shows an

inbred, thin-lipped, unsmiling, overfine face, with a tremendous beak of a Roman nose, and an air of hauteur which matches Sallust's description. Sallust, as Caesar's man, hated Cato, who opposed Caesar inflexibly, joined Pompey with reluctance, and was himself a sect. In self-discipline, endurance, oratorical and military skill he resembled his great-grandfather; the great difference lay in the influence upon the younger man of Greek philosophy, especially Stoicism. He consorted with philosophers—only for the sake of conversation with them would he indulge in wine—and imitated their simple life, going barefoot and dressing plainly. After Pompey's defeat and death, Cato, seeing that all was lost, resolved upon a Stoic suicide, attending first to the safety of those under his charge. On the night before he took his life, he conversed at length on philosophical subjects, read twice through Plato's *Phaedo* (on immortality), slept soundly, and then ripped out his bowels horribly with sword and hands. Caesar would have spared him; Cato scorned his mercy. With him died the best of the old Roman Republic.

A Strong-Minded Woman. The civil war which drove Cato to suicide evoked heroism in both sexes. One noble wife (*see Reading No. 6e*), perhaps named Turia, tracked down her parents' murderers, ransacked her jewel box to support her refugee husband, defended her villa from assault by slaves, and her inheritance from the designs of false guardians, saved her husband from the Second Trumvirate's proscriptions by hiding him between the roof and the ceiling of their bedroom, interceded for him with the sadistic triumvir Lepidus, and finally obtained for him Octavian's pardon. Only then could the pair enjoy a peaceful married life. Since they were childless, Turia even begged her husband to divorce her, a self-sacrificing proposal which left him almost speechless with indignation. He refused; she died before him; his funeral eulogy presents her as the best type of Roman matron: strong-minded, brave, practical, prudent. She is but one of a long gallery of strong-minded women, not all as chaste or as attractive as she: Brutus' mother, and perhaps Caesar's mistress, Servilia; Catullus' Lesbia; Cicero's shrewish wife Terentia; Augustus' redoubtable consort Livia and flamboyant daughter Julia; and the Agrippinas, Messalinas, and Poppaeas of the Empire.

A Sensible Prince. Republican propaganda under the Empire stereotyped Tiberius, Caligula, Claudius, and Nero as a hypocrite, a madman, a fool, and a rogue. The fool, Claudius, was alleged to be the catspaw of his freedmen and his wives. But inscriptions and papyri (*see Reading No. 6f*) have preserved enactments in his own unmistakable style, which show real grasp of, and offer workable solutions for, imperial problems. Livy, his master, had taught him that Rome had gradually extended her citizenship privileges. Claudius opened the Senate to wealthy Gauls and hoped to make it an empire-wide Parliament. His letter to Alexandria, rent by riots between Greeks and Jews, modestly deprecates Oriental adulation and in righteous wrath insists that the factions compose their differences: the Greeks are to allow the Jews freedom of worship: the Jews are to be content with the *status quo*. Though malicious gossip slandered Claudius in life, and a tasteless lampoon of Seneca's vilified him in death, his own words prove him a not unworthy pupil of one who saw virtue in the old Republic.

A Scholar. Romans admired and strove for encyclopaedic learning. Cicero eschewed long dinner parties, the dice board, and exercise to study and write philosophy. His older contemporary Varro, general, governor, antiquary, and librarian, left over three hundred volumes on everything human and divine. But, thanks to his letter-writing nephew, the best known of Roman encyclopaedists is Pliny the Elder, who, by the utmost parsimony of time in a busy life (*see Reading No. 6g*), produced, among much else, the fascinating hodgepodge of his *Natural History*, in thirty-seven books, embracing geography, anthropology, physiology, zoology, botany, poisons and their antidotes (knowledge especially useful under the Empire), mineralogy, metallurgy, and art history. His modest claim is to have handled 20,000 topics, drawn from 2,000 books by 473 authors, only 146 of them Roman. This life of harmless devotion to pedantic compiling was snuffed out by scientific curiosity combined with a desire to save human life. While serving (A.D. 79) as admiral at the naval station at Misenum across the Bay of Naples from Vesuvius, he sailed to get a closer view of the eruption and to save some stranded friends, and died of asphyxiation on the beach at Castellammare. His seventeen-year-old nephew, who preferred reading Livy to the excitement of volcanoes, survived to describe the scene in a letter to his friend the historian Tacitus.

Some Other Traits. The Roman character is too many-sided to be adequately summarized by any brief collection, however, picturesque, of characters remarkable for energetic devotion to state, family, personal ambition, or the intellectual life. Some discussion of the Romans' seamier side is in all honesty required; it follows in the next chapter. But among other characteristics worth mentioning are wit, hard-headedness, a streak of cruelty and conceit, and passion. Cicero, for example, was a famous wit. "If he were a cloaca," he said of a notorious braggart, "he would want to be the Cloaca Maxima." Caesar claimed to be able to tell a genuine from a spurious Ciceronian witticism. Hard-headedness is exemplified by the admiral who, when the sacred chickens refused to eat, threw them overboard, remarking, "If they will not eat, then let them drink!" We must consider the cruelty of the gladiatorial shows and the harmless vanity of the younger Pliny, boasting of his villas, benefactions, and crowded seven-hour orations. (Vergil, on the other hand, in his rare visits to Rome, used to hide in doorways for fear of being recognized.) And, finally, the passion of a Catullus, for friends, for poetry, for Lesbia, endures to remind us that Romans can be as attractive in their humanity as they are impressive when they are austere.

THE SEAMY SIDE

The Irresponsibles. The traditions recorded in the last chapter of self-restraint among the ruling class were more honored in the breach than the observance. The senatorial order, without the check imposed by a constitution providing a permanent loyal opposition, governed selfishly in its own interest. The middle class, of business men and tax-collectors, turned the Republic's wars and imperialist expansion into personal profit. And the Roman mob, discovering that its vote was worth money, subsisted on the dole and on bribes from candidates for office. The Republic ended in a chorus of laments about the decline from the good old days. The Julio-Claudian reforms improved matters for a while, especially in the provinces, but the Empire was vast, check-up difficult, and opportunities for chicanery correspondingly large. The swollen bureaucracy of the late Empire only meant more itching palms to grease. Honest provincial governors, like Cicero under the Republic, or the younger Pliny under the Empire, are frequent, but still too rare. In general, the old Roman governing class paid only lip service to the proposition that power brings responsibility, that *noblesse oblige*. Irresponsibly, they forfeited their rule to others more venal than themselves, failed to give the masses a stake in the government, or to educate them in good citizenship. Widespread political corruption and graft were the result.

Decline of Senatorial Government. In the Second Punic War (218-201 B.C.), Hannibal, the brilliant Carthaginian general, invaded Italy in the teeth of Roman armies often inadequately commanded by generals of the senatorial class. The result was widespread dissatisfaction in Rome and clamors from the plebs for breaking the monopoly of civil and military posts by members of patrician and plebeian wealthy families. Senatorial pussy-footing in the face of sensational war-contract frauds (*see Reading No. 7a*) exasperated the people into taking matters into their own hands. It was the plebeian tribunes, not the Senate, that tried to bring the rascally Postumius to book; the Senate contented itself with a vague resolution that the resulting riots were against the public interest and set a bad precedent. The Senate proved better at prophecy than at action. The war emergency brought to the fore the new commercial class of knights, of whom Postumius was one. Senators, barred by law from engaging in business, became behind-the-scenes backers of business deals, sometimes shady ones. Demagoguery grew rampant, and the Republic underwent the century of rioting and bloodbath called the Roman Revolution (133-31 B.C.).

Extortion Cases. Legislation like the Acilian Law against extortion suggests that all was not well with the Republic. (*See Reading No. 7b.*) The document is interesting also as showing the thoroughness and formalism of the Roman legal mind at work (*compare Reading No. 6a, and see Chapter 11*). The Acilian Law excluded senators from the juries set up to try extortion cases and replaced them with knights, who as tax-collectors had little interest in wiping out extortion in the provinces. The extortion court henceforward became the arena where political grudges were worked out. Formerly, with senators on juries, senatorial courtesy and log-rolling had made convictions practically impossible. Now that the knights had replaced them, they could penalize honest governors on trumped-up charges and safeguard their own gouging with the argument that they had to collect an extra percentage to cover their overhead. The Senate retaliated with the familiar political device of countering every left-wing bill with a promise to the people of something more attractive. The result was that by 111 B.C. the Acilian Law had become a dead letter, and by 81, senators were back on juries.

A Notorious Governor. Thanks to Cicero's tireless

energy in collecting evidence against him and to the diabolical detail with which he elaborated his charges, Gaius Verres (*see Reading No. 7c*) has become the most infamous name in the annals of rapacious Roman governors. He had learned the art of extortion under experts in the East, but escaped prosecution by turning state's evidence against his partner. His most lucrative area of operations, however, was Sicily, whose governorship he obtained by bribery (74 B.C.). Here he tampered ruinously with the vital grain supply, mulcted Sicilians on trumped-up charges, sometimes twice for the same alleged crime, slept with their wives, stole their art collections, falsified public records, sold priesthoods, robbed the customs office, and disgraced himself as general and as admiral. Cicero's evidence proved so overwhelming that the sinner decamped, and the prosecutor's speeches were never delivered in their entirety. Unwilling that so much hard work and brilliant rhetoric should be wasted, Cicero published them all as pamphlets. The reputation he won as a result stood him in good stead when he campaigned for the consulship seven years later.

How to Win Elections Without Actually Cheating. Since Cicero's chances of being elected consul were slim because no member of his family had ever held the office, he needed to conduct a particularly astute campaign. Although he probably knew enough about Roman politics to manage this unaided, his brother wrote for him a pamphlet on electioneering (*see Reading No. 7d*), a fascinating document in *Realpolitik*. Election depends, the pamphlet argues, on the people you know and the plain people you can persuade, by one means or another, to vote for you. All the familiar devices of modern campaigns are here; conciliating the ward bosses, making lavish promises (and actually fulfilling some of them), and surrounding oneself with crowds of supporters, those from the grass roots and those for whom the candidate has won lawsuits being counted upon to be especially enthusiastic. The candidate should have an elephant's memory (for names), entertain lavishly and systematically, keep the pork barrel open, assiduously circulate rumors damaging to his opponents, and, above all, be all things to all men. The pamphlet's closing picture of the Rome of 64 B.C. as a political jungle is illuminating and probably not exaggerated. The candidate was elected.

Subversion: Its Cause and Cure. Cicero's consulship proved no bed of roses. A disappointed candidate, Lucius Sergius Catilina, rallied disaffected elements (*see Reading No. 7e*) with the usual rabble-rousing agitation for canceling debts, a proposal which somehow always evokes more enthusiasm from the poor than from the propertied classes. Sallust's analysis of the subversive elements in Catiline's conspiracy is interesting especially because it shows no sympathy whatever for the legitimate grievances of the plebs, who got, in general, short shrift in Roman political theory and practice. In Rome a genuine split in principle between left and right was nonexistent; politics was a naked struggle for power in which the strong did what they could and the weak suffered what they must. Cicero, informed by spies of the conspiracy's course, declared a state of emergency. Catiline withdrew to his army waiting in Etruria and there fell in battle. Meanwhile, in Rome, Cicero, using his emergency powers, had some of the conspirators executed without trial, an act which was to plague him later, when his enemies accused him of unconstitutional conduct and drove him into temporary exile.

The Itching Palm. Civil war and political murder ran their brutal course; the Mediterranean world forfeited liberty for security and lived for two centuries under the Roman Peace. Literature preserves panegyrics of emperors; the sands of Egypt preserve scraps of papyrus, giving tantalizing glimpses of how the imperial administration looked to the man in the village street. The Egyptian community which kept the accounts presented here (*see Reading No. 7f*) took it for granted that the minor bureaucracy, civil and military, had to be paid protection money and softened with gifts: a suckling pig here, a flagon of wine there; it all helped. Even the money-changer took his percentage. In Asia Minor too, we find the imperial functionary with his hand out: here a village so impoverished by exactions (the Greek means exactly "shakedown," and occurs as early as St. Luke's Gospel, where Christ exhorts soldiers against the practice) that it cannot keep up its public bath; there a village where one paid to keep out of jail. Appeals to the Emperor brought temporary relief and new functionaries under new titles, but the abuse remained, as it still remains wherever half-educated civil servants put private profit before public duty.

The Black Market. Roman emperors, plagued by inflation, hoarding, and depression, resorted to debasing the coinage, in which the public soon lost confidence; the government itself came to prefer taxes in kind. The municipal ordinance here presented (*see Reading No. 7g*) was probably prompted by a new imperial issue of debased coins, which would produce a rush to exchange it for older, sounder currency—in the black market, since banks often closed down when new issues appeared, and refused to dip into their reserves. Local coinage, at a fixed exchange rate, was legal tender locally. Black-market speculators would buy up and hoard the undebased local currency, thus causing local inflation and interfering with local business. The city fathers hoped to cure the evil by leasing their exchange monopoly to a single local banker. The document is interesting also as the latest known example of municipal independence under the Empire: here the city still imposes the penalties, and its magistrates still administer the law, but behind them looms the shadow of their "most divine masters, the Emperors."

Morality by the Book. The promulgation in Rome, on Christmas day, A.D. 438, of the Theodosian Code, embodying 126 years of imperial edicts, evoked no less than forty-three senatorial acclamations, each repeated eight to twenty-eight times. The wildest enthusiasm greeted the Code's renewed provisions against bureaucratic corruption. Diocletian (A.D. 284-305) had shored up the massive, tottering imperial fabric with an incredibly complex and repressive administrative hierarchy, with supersecret police to spy on secret police, and corruption everywhere. The individual citizen had to bribe petty clerks to see a judge, a governor, or even an official record. Since the document presented here (*see Reading No. 7h*) was already over a century old when the Code was promulgated, we must assume that the Code's perplexed rhetoric had not sufficed to right the wrongs it fulminated against. The petty bureaucrats' victims, father and son bound to farm or city labor, fleeced by tax-gatherers, dragooned by recruiting officers, educated to submit abjectly to authority, turned willingly to the barbarian invader as the lesser evil. Already we are in the atmosphere of the Middle Ages.

— 8 —

CONSERVATISM REVISITED

The Idea of Aristocracy. "I suppose it would be true to say," Charles Eliot Norton used to tell his Harvard classes, "that none of you has ever seen an aristocrat." Nowadays, plutocracy—symbolized by solid gold Cadillacs, swimming pools, and mink coats—is often confused with aristocracy, and the Roman equivalents of these symbols are not hard to find. But the Romans cherished an ideal of the best, however little they exemplified it in practice. Its intellectual pedigree is partly Greek, partly indigenous, and it perhaps differs enough from ours to deserve some elaboration. For a Roman, aristocracy is primarily a political concept: government is more important than business; indeed most business, especially small business, is vulgar. Aristocracy is government by the intellectually and morally best, in the interest of the governed. Romans generally accepted "best" and "conservative" as synonyms; Cicero intellectualized the concept of conservatism. Good government is therefore intelligent conservative government, in the early Republic a matter of tradition, which was best preserved in old landed families. Therefore, rule by persons of property, pedigree, and intelligence is best; these three, but the greatest of these is intelligence. Excellence is also a matter of efficiency, in war, victory, politics, begetting children, and, incidentally, honest money-making. (*See Reading No. 8a.*) Noble families are expected to show a social conscience, to go into government and not shame their ancestors. The ideal repository of aristocratic excellence is the Senate. When aristocratic ranks are thinned, or aristocratic policy doubted, skilled propagandists must persuade

53

wide segments of the population that their interests are identical with those of the intellectual élite, who do their hard thinking for them and leave them free for business as usual. Checking ballots will quickly reveal to a vigilant aristocracy which elements of the citizenry fail to appreciate their blessings. The saving grace of these concepts, which are hardly those most Americans learn at their mother's knee, is the notion that *noblesse oblige:* the aristocracy forfeits its privilege when it ceases to govern intelligently in the people's interest. But there is a missing element: the people are not to be trusted to define their own interest; there is no scope for popular initiative.

The "Family Compact." Of all Roman aristocratic clans none had more distinguished annals than the Fabii. (*See Reading No. 8b.*) The writing of a history of Rome, now lost, by a member of the clan did nothing to dispel this impression. Livy's story of the Fabian clan's single-handed war with Veii probably comes from Fabius Pictor's history. The Fabii were ambushed and died fighting, almost to a man. But one survived, enough to continue the clan's traditions. In the fourth century B.C. the Fabii contrived to pass the consulship from father to son for three generations, and in the Second Punic War a Fabius fought against Hannibal a delaying action which George Washington imitated against the British in the American Revolution. Over seventy Fabii served the Republic. They are evenly divided over the centuries; race suicide, the plague of other aristocratic families, did not thin their ranks. By intermarriages, this and other noble clans still further protected their stake in the nation throughout Republican history. When they failed to measure up to tradition, a new concept of intellectual aristocracy emerged.

A Senate of Kings. Polybius' analysis of the causes of Rome's greatness proceeds on the theory that Rome blended the best of three kinds of constitutions: monarchy in the consuls, aristocracy in the Senate, democracy in the people. But his treatment (*see Reading No. 8c*) does not conceal the aristocratic Senate's predominance. In Rome, officeholding ennobled the holders and entitled them, when their year in office was over, to places in the Senate, from which they controlled finance, the courts, foreign relations, war and peace, quite independently of the people, who had originally elected them. But Polybius, perhaps exasperated by Rome's shift in the mid-second century from protectorate to conquest of his homeland, sees seeds of degeneracy in the Senate, and, indeed, from the Gracchan age onward its prestige dwindles as that of the military leaders rises. To say that the Roman Republic collapsed when military leaders destroyed the Senate's authority is only part of the truth. Aristocracy and conservatism must always be vigilant against a tendency to hardening of the arteries and fossilization; aristocrats in the Senate refused to reform the order from within, or to tolerate brilliant equals like Julius Caesar. Caesar also spoke part of the truth when he said after defeating the senatorial forces at Pharsalus (48 B.C.), "They would have it so."

Conservatism for All. The world's most eloquent spokesman for conservatism is Cicero; it is ironic that modern Republican party leaders read him so little. Returning from exile in 57 B.C., he found the *populares* (*see Reading No. 8d*) in the ascendant; Caesar carrying all before him in Gaul; Caesar, Pompey, and Crassus dividing the world among them. Cicero, himself not of aristocratic birth, judged it time to break the old aristocratic narrowness (which he accurately judged responsible for his own misfortunes), and invite all comers, or all who could show a patent of respectability, to join the banner of a New Conservatism. He appeals especially to small town civic leaders, country squires, businessmen, and the young (the defense in court of a young man, Sestius, is the occasion of his rallying-cry). His slogan, "Peace with Honor," implies security for business and support for his own ambitions to return to political power. For there can be little doubt that he sees himself as *princeps*, "initiator of public policy," director of the New Conservatism; it is another irony that when the *princeps* came he was Octavian-Augustus, who connived at Cicero's murder. The traditionalism of Cicero's platform is significant; the state religion will, as before, further *optimates'* policies and frustrate the knavish tricks of radicals; a sound economy (to appeal to the knights, his own class) rests, in his view, on an honest imperialism.

An Aristocracy of Intellect. Four years after *For Sestius,* Cicero published a political manifesto, his *Republic,* creatively borrowing from Plato and Aristotle and applying his findings in the Roman way to contemporary conditions. Monarchy is the ideal, but monarchs are fallible; democracy is unthinkable, for the people quarrel and lack vision. These are the extremes; the mean, where virtue lies, is an intellectual aristocracy, an elite of *principes.* With a *princeps* at the helm, ordinary Romans can sleep quietly in their beds and let the *princeps* have the headaches. Neither Cicero nor any other ancient political theorist takes the masses into account; their job is to do exactly what their leaders tell them to. As long as the *principes* know and do their duty, Cicero thinks the plebs have nothing to lose. What the plebs thought is not recorded. Like George Orwell's pigs, though with much better intentions, Cicero holds that all men are equal, but some are more equal than others. He thinks it unfair that inferior intellects should govern superior ones. For intellect, initiative, and political foresight are the core of Cicero's New Conservatism; the old aristocracy of pedigree is intellectually bankrupt. The new *princeps* is to be an initiator, a reformer; his prestige, based on reform, excludes both old guard and new nabobs. Pompey might have been *princeps,* but he was a bumbler; Caesar's immoderate ambition rules him out. Cicero never found a *princeps* and never became one, but his ideas bore fruit in the man who did.

The New Conservatism and Natural Law. Cicero's *Republic,* like Plato's, was followed by his *Laws* (about 52-46 B.C.; never finished), which idealize actual Roman law as his *Republic* idealized the actual constitution. Here Cicero adapts his laws to the *princeps*-directed state, and popularizes for all succeeding ages some fundamental ideas of western legal and political theory (*see Reading No. 8f*): Stoic concepts like natural law, which underlies the American Declaration of Independence; or the law of nations, which underlies man's aspirations towards one world. Both concepts stem from the Greek view of man as a rational animal, deriving his reason from God and sharing it with all other men, who are therefore his brothers, and to be treated with equity. But man's reason places him high in the hierarchy of nature, in the Great Chain of Being which rises from stocks and stones and worse than senseless things through Man Thinking to God. Man Thinking is the *princeps;* his exalted place in Nature's order justifies the exalted place reserved for him in the state by the New Conservatism. Neither the unreconstructed old aristocracy of pedigree nor the unintelligent plebs has so high a place in nature as the new, intellectual *princeps* has; therefore, neither deserves so high a place in the state. The reformed Republic will be the *princeps'* directive intelligence in action; the vision of one universal state is the vision of a Roman Empire reformed by directive intelligence. The vision was in part realized by Augustus' administrative reforms in the Roman provinces.

How to Control the Popular Vote. Cicero was no more a liberal democrat than our own Founding Fathers. That the benevolent rule of an intellectual élite, which he desiderates, should be frustrated by the bought votes of an untutored mob seemed to him intolerable. A ballot the plebs shall have, for they are fellow rational animals, albeit of an inferior order of intelligence, and deserve to be fairly treated. But a secret ballot (*see Reading No. 8g*) would give them the power to pervert the *princeps'* directive intelligence and prevent, irrationally, indispensable reforms. Safeguards at the polls are essential, to stop election fraud, but the present laws do not even prevent this. Instead, either the Old Guard may be fraudulently elected, or the plebs may, with the secret ballot, reject a candidate of the New Conservatism. Therefore, let the ballot be open to inspection by "any really substantial aristocratic citizen"; i.e., by intellectuals like-minded with Cicero. Thereby the plebs will find favor with the New Conservatives, whose service is perfect freedom. All this close reasoning, based on a lack of faith in the people well calculated to make a liberal's blood run cold, is justified in Cicero's mind by his trust in the social conscience of the intellectual in office and his realistic assessment of the limitations of the Roman mob, whom generations of oligarchic rule had left without adequate political experience.

Vulgar and Gentlemanly Occupations. Greek ide-

alistic dualism, to which Cicero subscribed, made value
judgments exalting mind over matter, reason (in *principes*) over emotion (in common men), and by inference
(*see Reading No. 8h*), mental over physical work. In
general, work for pay is considered socially degrading, the
luxury trades particularly so, for the doctrine is Stoic,
and the Stoics were Puritans. Cicero distinguishes between
vulgar and gentlemanly occupations in *On Duty,* a long
letter to his son, happily undutiful as a student in Athens.
The theme, as usual, is *noblesse oblige:* the intellectual
aristocracy has a duty; it must govern, according to the
four cardinal virtues, as wisely, justly, bravely, and tem-
perately as it can. Temperance includes decorum, a thoroughly Roman concept; it embraces dressing plainly,
practicing self-control, not gossiping, not doing eccentric
things "like singing in the Forum." In this context un-
gentlemanly occupations are discussed. The idea that
bigness makes business respectable reflects little credit
either on Cicero or on big business; it may be Cicero's
bid for support for the New Conservatism from the
knights. The high esteem of farming is, like the idea of
decorum, thoroughly Roman; it is further discussed in
Chapter 10. Doctors, architects, and professors of the
liberal arts may derive some satisfaction from their high
place in Cicero's esteem, but, in general, the snobbishness
involved may well seem to many one of the more pernicious of our legacies from Rome.

RELIGION AND PHILOSOPHY

Formalism. Roman religion is a paradox: at once conservative in ritual (*see Reading No. 9a*), and innovating in its hospitality to foreign cults. It grew to be Greek in outward semblance but remained primitive at the core. (*See Reading No. 9b.*) Festivals like the Lupercalia preserve primitive fertility rites; at the Saturnalia, relic of simpler days, slaves exchanged places with their masters; the date, the merriment, and the exchange of gifts survive in modern Christmas. To a Roman, religion was a contractual relation between him and his gods; he scratched their backs and expected them to scratch his. In religion as in literature, Romans borrowed creatively: gods originally native keep their personality; Greek gods undergo strong local influence. The state religion was cold, abstract, and formal, involving no participation whatever by the worshiper in the service. Religion imported from the Greek East was warmer and more emotional; from the East was to come the religion that would silence the pagan cults forever (*see Chapter 13*). As ancestor-worshipers the Romans were downright Japanese; at funerals modern men wore the masks of their ancestors. Roman religion, without theological dogma or ethical code, was not proof against the temptations which beset its votaries when they became enormously rich, or powerful, or skeptical, or starved for a stronger emotional outlet than it could or would provide. And so it was reduced to a shaky façade masking a spiritual void.

Political Manipulation. Official Roman religion was inseparably bound up with politics. The *pontifex maxi-*

mus, head of a powerful board of religious advisers to the consuls, was elected, as were the augurs and the board for consulting the Sibylline books. Until 300 B.C. the Chief Pontiff was always a patrician, after that date frequently so. Of the seventeen Chief Pontiffs 253-12 B.C., seven were patricians, and all had been consuls. To be elected required political manipulation; after election these secular priests meddled further in politics. Jupiter's priest, the *flamen Dialis,* was so hedged about with taboos that appointment to this post was political annihilation; the *optimates* almost maneuvered Julius Caesar into it, and Roman history would have been very different if they had succeeded. The augurs, observing omens from lightning, quadrupeds, portents, flights of birds, and the feeding of the sacred chickens, interpreted according to secret rules the gods' will regarding any proposed political action. The opportunity for manipulation is obvious. The *optimates* acquiesced in religious thanksgivings of unprecedented length for Julius Caesar; they knew that as long as the festival lasted their enemy could call no popular assembly for the passage of radical legislation. Polybius' rationalistic, aristocratic comment (*see Reading No. 9c*) surely reflects his conversations with the ruling class, who valued the impact upon the mob mind of solemn religious processions, and the deterrent effect of threats of hell-fire and brimstone.

Religion and Superstition. A religious system like Rome's, politically manipulated and dedicated to "protecting ancestral institutions by retaining old rites" (*see Reading No. 9d*) positively encouraged superstition, at least among the less sophisticated; and where the state religion left off, irresponsible impostors began. Hedge priests peddled oracles, uttered prophecies, and interpreted both dreams and the results of drawing lots. Omens were derived from comets (as at Caesar's death), eclipses and meteors (as during Catiline's conspiracy), an ape crossing one's path, a sneeze, a twitch, or any involuntary act or utterance interpreted as significant in a way not realized by the doer. Astrologers read horoscopes. Diviners (*haruspices*) inspected animal livers, noted thunder on the left, and kept records, which survive, of births of two-headed calves, streams running blood, statues sweating.

Magic charms, uttered in gibberish, would catch a thief; fantastically detailed curses, inscribed on lead, would make a charioteer lose a race. There were skeptics: Cicero wonders how one *haruspex* can pass another without laughing in his face; the Epicurean poet Lucretius calls Jupiter a very bad shot, to strike his own temples with lightning so often; occasional tomb inscriptions scoff at hell or mock at Fortune. Superstition is one of the failings that make the Romans interesting and much like us. Only those who have never knocked wood, shot dice, bought a lottery ticket, had tea leaves, their palms, or their horoscopes read, or bet on a horse race will condemn without understanding.

Emperor Worship, especially of bad emperors, is really an index to the essential irreligiosity of the Roman mind. Ruler cult came to Rome from the Greek East, a heritage from pharaohs, Alexander the Great, and the Ptolemies. Romulus' apotheosis (*see Reading No. 1a*) was a late, Greek-influenced invention. Greeks honored Romans like Scipio the Elder and the "liberator" Flamininus as divine. Julius Caesar had been augur and Chief Pontiff; he was deified after his murder, with his own temple, priest (who appears on the relief of the Altar of Peace), and festival. Henceforward, controlled by a supreme ruler, the state religion functioned to support a monarch numbered among the gods of the state. Augustus was never worshiped in Italy during his lifetime, but he encouraged provincial cults of his attendant spirit or *genius*. His deification by the Senate after his death (*see Reading No. 9e*) set a precedent. The Greek East worshiped Tiberius and Claudius despite their deprecations. Caligula, who was only mad nor'-nor' east, admitted that he felt godhood stealing over him. Seneca calls the deification of the somewhat grotesque Claudius "pumpkinification." Nero's voice was regarded as divine. Questions of the sincerity of emperor worship, its spontaneity, or satisfaction of religious need are perhaps better not raised, but political significance it certainly had, as an expression of loyalty and solidarity, and as an outlet, in cult service, for humble folk's frustrated political ambitions. Christian refusal to worship emperors' statues provoked persecutions; when Christianity triumphed, the god-emperor became instead the protected of God; thus one fruit of emperor worship is the doctrine of the divine right of kings.

Philosophy: Epicureanism and Its Critics. For pure philosophical speculation, especially metaphysics, the practical Roman mind had no taste. Applied philosophy, especially ethics and politics, was another matter. Epicureanism, creatively borrowed from the Greeks, had a practical appeal. Epicurus advocated the study of atomic physics not for its own sake, nor for the sake of blowing one's fellow man to atoms, but to rid mankind of the fear of the gods and of death (*see The Greek Mind, p. 82*). The most eloquent Roman Epicurean was the poet Lucretius (about 94-55 B.C.), who has been called, "for majesty of theme, . . . sustained eloquence of exposition, acuteness of philosophical insight and argumentation, poetic imagery and musical cadence, and sheer enthusiasm of scientific passion . . . the greatest poet that ever lived." His epic, *On the Nature of Things,* makes high poetry of concepts never before poetically treated: atomic kinds, shapes, and movements, psychology of sensation and thought, origin of species, survival of the fittest, primitive man and his culture, the nature of phenomena in earth and heaven. But its core is the detailed argument that an awareness of our atomic structure, which, being composite, will inevitably decompose, will free us from fear of death. (*See Reading No. 9f.*) When we are, death is not; when death is, we are not. Lucretius' conclusion is that we should not worry; atomic physics will bring us peace of mind.

Epicureans in theory abstained from politics; their opponents criticized this as not the Roman way. Cicero is especially savage against Epicureans (*see Reading No. 9g*), particularly their ethics and physics. Epicurean ethics held that desire for pleasure, qualified importantly as that of a wise man, is the best incentive to good conduct. Epicurean physics, with its "rush-hour crowd of atoms," undoes the Great Chain of Being. So, in an ethics in which each man is invited to consult his own interest, emotion counts, and self-sacrificing Roman Puritans are not admired. A world view involving no value judgments cut at the base of the collectivist, hierarchical structure

RELIGION AND PHILOSOPHY   63

on which rested the New Conservatism. Stoicism suited
Cicero's book much better, or Aristotelianism, which
could be manipulated to place the *princeps* in a mean
between extremes. Personally, Cicero was attracted by
the Academics, skeptics who advocated suspension of
judgment. Cicero actually calls Epicureanism subversive,
since, he argues, it destroys that desire to give and receive
benefits on which depends the harmonious working of
the New Conservatism among senators, knights, and
plebs. Epicureans mocked the politically manipulated
state religion, too. An Epicurean god, made in their own
image, would take no pleasure in the vexations of administering a universe. On disbelief in administrative gods
follows disbelief in administrative *principes;* no wonder
Cicero is angry! His victim, Piso, was Caesar's father-in-
law; in his family villa at Herculaneum, a whole Epicurean library has been found.

Stoicism affected Rome as early as Tiberius Gracchus' time. The Stoics Panaetius and Posidonius profoundly influenced Cicero; a blind Stoic, Diodotus, lived
in Cicero's house; Cicero's philosophical essays discuss
Stoicism exhaustively. Its appeal was wide: under the
Empire the major Stoics were a courtier (Seneca: *see
Reading No. 9h*), a slave (Epictetus), and an emperor
(Marcus Aurelius: *see Reading No. 9i*). Most voluminous
is Seneca (4 B.C.-A.D. 65), who attacked luxury from
the lap of luxury, was Nero's tutor, and finally, in a
Stoic suicide, became his victim. Seneca is full of Stoic
adjurations to follow nature, scorn fortune, despise hope,
bear adversity, defy disaster, fight luxury, purify the mind,
avoid profiteering, court freedom, and, when all else fails,
cut the cable. No one would guess from his barbaric
yawps that Stoicism was an orderly system. Its ethics
make virtue the chief end; the sage, choosing between
good and evil, lives in conformity to Nature; (i.e., universal, controlling Reason), and contracts his desires to
fit his means. Stoics fear death no more than Epicureans,
but for a different reason: Stoics believe in immortality;
Stoic physics is based upon the Great Chain of Being
and the Argument from Design: the heavens declare the
glory of God; the firmament showeth his handiwork.
The Stoic universe runs in cycles, each ending in a great

fire. Perhaps the most important influence of Roman Stoicism was its humanizing effect upon Roman law. (*See Chapter 11.*)

The Romans as Philosophers. Roman philosophy, like American, originated little, and its main strength lies, paradoxically, in what may be called idealistic pragmatism: Platonic dualism applied to concrete situations, especially in politics. Of the three major philosophers in Latin (Epictetus and Marcus Aurelius wrote in Greek), Lucretius the materialist left no followers; Seneca the Stoic is more influential as a tragic poet, and more interesting as a neurotic, than as a philosopher. Cicero remains. His motives for philosophizing are very Roman: intellectual curiosity, consolation in adversity, occupation for leisure, desire to popularize, but above all to propagandize, in two ways: first, to prove that Latin is as good a philosophical vehicle as Greek (Cicero invented the Western world's philosophical vocabulary; "quality," for instance, is a word of his coining); second, to justify the political role of the New Conservatism. A work of his converted St. Augustine. St. Ambrose adapted his *On Duty* to the Christian priesthood. St. Thomas Aquinas borrowed from him on natural law. The great international lawyer Hugo Grotius was indebted to Cicero's interpretation of Stoicism. And American Federalists used Cicero when they framed the Constitution. His philosophy, then, forms the cornerstone of the conservative tradition; the durability of that cornerstone is one of the burning questions of our troubled time.

— 10 —

THE ROMANS AND THE LAND

Rome's Primarily Agricultural Economy is extensively reflected in Latin literature, and attention must be paid to it by all who would understand the Roman mind at work. Agricultural festivals form the backbone of the religious calendar. Latin is a no-nonsense, farmer's language; its metaphors, nomenclature, and vocabulary are agricultural. Rome's earliest law is farmer's law. Roman conservatism is something a Maine or Wisconsin farmer may sympathize with, and reflect in his voting. Embattled farmers made the Roman Republic; landholding was the qualification for citizenship, farming the most respected occupation. From the mid-second century B.C. large estates were the rule, and absentee ownership, sharecroppers, and slave labor all created problems. After the Roman Revolution, swords were beaten into ploughshares, and the farmer's life was idealized. Under the Empire, small holdings on large estates were increasingly leased to free tenant farmers, eventually bound to their land as on medieval manors. To illuminate all this we have the old-fashioned horse sense of Cato the Elder, the rigid schematics of Varro, the high poetry with which Vergil's *Georgics* invest the smallest detail of the farmer's life, and the lucid practicality of Columella. Love of the land, and determination to farm it well link the ancient Roman to the modern Italian *contadino,* the English country squire of day before yesterday, or the American dreaming of a farm to retire to.

Capital Farming. Cato, despite his old-fashioned lore, was an up-to-date capital farmer. (*See Reading No. 10a.*) His work is a farmer's notebook of random jottings useful to the writer, his friends, and his neighbors. Its severe simplicity, reflected especially in its fascinating lists of charms, recipes, and household remedies, recalls the good old days of the early Republic which Romans thought they remembered. But the farm Cato has in mind is a modern one, irrigated and planted to olives, vines, orchard, and pasture. (*See Reading No. 10b.*) It is run by an overseer, with his wife as housekeeper. There are share-croppers on the land, and large gangs of slaves who are worked hard and fed and clothed with skinflint parsimony: sour wine; a cloak, blanket, and shoes every two years, the old clothes to be turned in for patchwork. There is work and to spare for all; tasks are prescribed for evenings, winter, and rainy days. The farm is as far as possible self-supporting, with its own lime kilns, tile factory, and woodlot, but good markets are listed for buying and selling.

Land Grants for Veterans. The ranks of the re-formed Marian army (*see Chapter 4*) were landless. Promise of land grants as a reward for service was a great inducement. But just when demand for land was at its height, available public land in Italy was at a minimum. The alternatives were confiscation, purchase, or overseas colonization. Confiscation was the price many Italian landholders paid for betting on the wrong side in the Roman Revolution. Even Vergil escaped losing his Po valley farm only by personal intercession with Octavian, whose schoolfellow he had been. The less fortunate might have to go as refugees to start life over again in far places: Africa, Scythia, Crete, or Britain. Appian, who wrote under Antoninus Pius (A.D. 138-161) from anti-Augustan sources, sympathizes with the under-dog (*see Reading No. 10c*); his picture of Roman legion-naires settled about the countryside ready to pounce on subversion is perhaps overdrawn. Augustus in fact aimed at rehabilitating Italy, ravaged by a century of civil wars. His back-to-the-land movement worked hardships, but it made Italy flourish. To help the new farmers find their feet and to revive interest in country life, Varro in prose, and Vergil in great poetry, wrote farmers' hand-books, the latter at least encouraged by the régime.

Varro had a systematic, practical mind. His three

books *On Agriculture* are divided and subdivided in a
professorial way. A generation later, Ovid, wickedly
parodying this orderliness, similarly divided and subdivided *The Art of Love*. In jest or in earnest, this is the
way the Roman mind works. Varro's three books discuss
dirt farming (*see Reading No. 10d*), animal husbandry,
and raising birds, game, bees, and fish for profit. They
are utterly practical throughout, with no words wasted on
beauties of nature, jollity at harvest time, or the rights
of man. The dirt farmer learns, inexorably, about four
kinds of vine props, ninety-nine kinds of soil, four types
of enclosures (including rail fences and stone walls);
about farmhands, animals, and tools, with orderly detail
about preparing, planting, cultivating, harvesting, storing,
and marketing the crop. The animal-husbandry section
distinguishes nine kinds of animals: sheep, goats, pigs,
oxen, asses, horses, mules, dogs, and herdsmen. (The latter
may have their mates with them to keep them contented.)
The last book describes an aviary (small birds fetch large
profits); an apiary (with comment on the humanlike
qualities of bees); and fish ponds, whose masters worry
as much about ailing fish as about ailing slaves. It would
take more than this to make farming seem attractive.

Vergil supplied the something more. Himself a
farmer's son, he knows, better than Varro, his four chosen
subjects: the farmer's tasks, trees and vines, horses and
cattle, and bees. More than that, he loves them, seeing
in them things forever meaningful to man; in Vergil,
"the poetry of earth is never dead." So his four books,
though crammed with facts, tell, at a deeper level, of the
dignity of man's labor, nature's luxuriance, love and
death (in stallions breeding and cattle dying of murrain),
and immortality and chastity (in the life of the bee).
Work is hard, nature inconstant, but there are blessings to
count: the loveliness of Italy, peace after struggle, rich-
ness of harvest, pleasure in family and friends. (*See
Reading No. 10e.*) And perhaps his bees, with their drive,
their orderliness, and their lack of freedom, struck the
more sensitive of his Roman readers as themselves writ
small. His work weds science and art. He discusses tech-
nicalities without being dull, he uses Hesiod and Cato
without being derivative. He fashions his line patterns

with loving care: that of Book IV is 7-141-132-134-143-8. Combining practicality with poetry, remaking tradition into something new and fresh, he is the exemplar of the Roman mind at its best.

Columella. Vergil left unfulfilled a promise to treat of flower gardens. Columella, author of twelve books in prose *On Agriculture,* bursts into verse at one point to describe them. The passage, with its cordial invitation of the nymphs to a picnic (*see Reading No. 10f*), is pleasant versification, not great poetry. Columella's forte is science. Like Varro, he condemns the importation of grain. He treats the same subjects as Cato, Varro, and Vergil, but at greater length, devoting, for example, two whole books to the duties of the overseer and his wife. The overseer should be a middle-aged paragon, steady, loyal, familiar with ploughing, digging, mowing, forestry, vine-dressing, veterinary science, and sheep-herding; not too intimate with the hands, but a good judge of which have brawn and which brains. Of sleep, wine-bibbing, love-making, and little trips to town he must be equally abstemious. He must set the example for briskness and industry, keep the hands healthy, use his holidays to check inventory of tools both mute and vocal. His wife, fit helpmeet, has charge of storeroom and pantry, woolwork, housecleaning, and putting up preserves. As he must show in his humble station a good governor's virtues, so she must embody those, now rare, of the Roman matron of the good old days.

Roman Farming and Imperial Civilization. Columella's bailiff and his wife are not fictional characters. In an age when Rome, as Tacitus, Suetonius, and Juvenal describe it, was full of effeminate, vicious men, and domineering, extravagant, and equally vicious women, the countryside had its quota of such steady, salt-of-the-earth couples as this, preserving in reality the sometimes mythical virtues of the old Republic. They are the stuff Gibbon's happy age of the Antonines was made of. Their virtues must have made even the large estates of which Pliny complains (*see Reading No. 10g*) more bearable. Rome was within a generation of her millennium when a Christian, Tertullian (*see Reading No. 10h*), surely not an overfriendly witness, was moved to language as laudatory as Aelius Aristides' (*see Reading No 3i*) as he describes the world-wide civilizing effect of Roman agriculture. The passage is of course rhetorical and over-blown, and in context its purpose is not to praise Rome, but to disprove the pagan doctrine of metempsychosis. But there is truth in it. Behind the tax-gatherer and the money-lender, the venal bureaucrat and the brutal soldier, life on the land went on, not always happily, but not always despairingly either. And from start to finish, enough Romans had honest dirt under their fingernails to keep the world going, sane and civilized, rather better than worse off under the sober sway of Roman law.

— 11 —

ROMAN LAW

Civilizing Influence of Roman Law. Rome's legal system, gradually evolved, was, for the Roman man of property and his retainers, the best instrument for securing justice, and perhaps the greatest achievement of the Roman mind. Modern liberals must remember that Romans took the distinction between upper and lower classes as a fact of life, though as they contemplate the monolithic structure of Roman law they may find it difficult to forget a famous remark about "the majestic equity of the Law, which forbids rich and poor alike to sleep under bridges." The following paragraphs recognize Roman class distinctions as a historical fact, without accepting them as a moral principle. Roman law at its best evinces a spirit of honor, good faith, and equitable firmness (*see Reading No. 11a*) unsurpassed even in English common law. Among its civilizing influences were the principle that no man should be judged guilty until after the facts were examined. As St. Paul knew (*see Reading No. 11b*), Romans never condemned a man without letting him face his accusers and defend himself. In some lawsuits both parties had equal legal responsibility to furnish bond in the same amount, implying the principle of presumption of innocence until guilt is proven. Roman courts gave defendants the advantage. (*See Reading No. 11c.*) The men of property who signed the Declaration of Independence, in affirming that all men are created equal, stated a principle of Roman law. The Roman lawyers' view that no law is binding unless founded on reason was used as an argument against the Prohibition Amendment. In constitutional law, modern deliberative assemblies,

70

except in the United States, follow the Roman rule: in a conflict of laws, the latest one is binding. Finally, in Roman legal theory the people delegated the emperor's powers to him; hence the statement in the Declaration of Independence that governments derive "their just powers from the consent of the governed."

Early Roman Law.   Roman law sprang from three main sources: civil law, the law of nations, and natural law (*see Reading No. 11d*), all, by Cicero's time, operating concurrently. The XII Tables (*see Reading No. 11e*) exemplify the civil law; they codify legal customs mostly inherited from the monarchy. Their precision, clarity, brevity, and force presuppose long experience in legal science. The people, Senate, and magistrates supplemented them with laws and plebiscites, resolutions, and edicts; the emperors added decrees, decisions in court, answers on points of law, and instructions to officials.

The Urban Praetor interpreted the law. On entering office he listed in an edict the principles he intended to follow, including the XII Tables and later Republican legislative enactments. He was not a trial judge, but a chief justice to whom both sides submitted their arguments. He sought agreement between the parties on the point of law on which they wanted their case tried; failing agreement, both parties were bound by his choice. Then the parties (or, failing agreement, the praetor) appointed as judge a senator or knight, not a professional lawyer; that class did not yet exist. Advisers somewhat like our jury assisted him to decide whether the facts presented fell under the point of law indicated by the praetor. If not, the defendant was declared not guilty. Procedure was much more rapid than in the modern American hierarchy of courts. Since the urban praetor might freely select his edict's principles, he could, if he chose, modernize, humanize, or liberalize the law. The praetorship was elective, eventually open to plebeians. A liberal program enunciated by a plebeian who had not sold himself to the reactionaries might draw more votes.

The Jurisprudents.   The praetor sought guidance from the best available legal minds. Though the early and middle Republic had no professional lawyers, an authoritative class of "jurisprudents" had grown up (*see Reading No. 11f*), mostly ex-pontiffs, magistrates, judges, or advisers to praetors or judges, with experience as defenders of their own families' clients. Since nearly all were senators, their experience helped to formulate Senate enactments and influence magistrates' judgment. In various ways these experts recorded their own pragmatic approach to legal questions, and thus a legal philosophy grew up. Jurisprudents continued to help Roman law develop down into the late Empire.

The Law of Nations. The appointment, about 242 B.C. (*see Reading No. 11g*), of a special praetor for foreigners opened a new era in Roman law's development. Whereas the modern state subjects all immigrants and visitors to its own laws, the Romans created for such persons a new legal system combining simplicity with fairness. Foreigners ignorant of Latin did not have to plead in the archaic formulae of the XII Tables. (In Rome all litigants pleaded their own cases.) The praetor for foreigners interpreted not the letter but the spirit of the law, invoking broad concepts like intent, good faith, or fair play. These gradually superseded the maze of national legal practices to create a new law of nations (*see Reading No. 11h*), equitable to all. Thus was invented, partly by creative borrowing from Hellenistic law, a new legal concept—equity, the spirit of enlightened justice, sensitive to circumstances, assisting rather than dictating, preventing rather than punishing, flexible and humane. These principles came to be applied also by the urban praetor, and all over the Empire. After A.D. 212, when Caracalla made all foreigners citizens, the whole empire lived under the civil law as penetrated by the philosophy and provisions of the law of nations.

Natural Law was a third element in Roman law's development. Cicero, as we saw, popularized in the Latin West the Stoic idea of natural law, where nature is identified with God. He argued that law was no mere piece of human ingenuity or ordinary legislation, but something eternal, that rules the whole universe. True law is directive intelligence, agreeing with nature, universal in application, unchanging, everlasting; a definition which does the New Conservatism no harm. The concept influenced both the Christian church and English common law, and, through the latter, the "self-evident truths" on the "laws of Nature and of Nature's God" mentioned in the Declaration of Independence. The United States Supreme Court has repeatedly affirmed the principle that reason and natural law are the ultimate standards of legal judgment. The concept of natural law reinvigorated the Romans' quest for higher principles of justice; slavery, for example, was declared unnatural. Though there were no Roman abolitionists, the slave's lot was at least improved (*see Reading No. 11i*), and the whole imperial concept of justice subtly humanized, especially through the unofficial but nonetheless real influence of natural law upon the self-perpetuating praetor's edict.

The Jurists. In their judicial capacity the emperors sought guidance from the best legal minds of the day. Roman jurisprudence developed steadily for five hundred years, from mid-Republic to mid-Empire, flowering in the second and early third centuries A.D. It did not merely educate students in legal tricks; it gave them a deeper understanding of the spirit or philosophy of the law, creating in the process a science of the just and the equitable. Roman jurists could do this because magistrates regularly and sensibly invited them to sit as advisers in their councils—an innovation in world history—, because the penetrating Roman legal mind had a gift for generalizing or theorizing from masses of individual enactments, and because the art of government was in the Roman blood, and a set of rules was a practical help. Jurists advising trial judges helped to shape individual edicts and other legislation, and to guide the court's verdict. Thus jurists could accommodate old laws and interpretations to the changing present, reorienting the civil law toward the liberalism of the law of nations and the higher morality of natural law, and fusing all three into one universal law. Jurists produced quantities of *Digests, Institutes,* and other works invaluable for legal history and for the exposition of the spirit of the law. Written lucidly, forcefully and concisely, these are the most original branch of Silver Latin. Penetrating and scholarly, but without arrogance, they seek always the formulae or opinions most conducive to attaining justice.

Jurists on the Privy Council. Like their Republican predecessors, but more actively, the imperial jurisprudents drafted laws and formulated verdicts. They regularly achieved magistracies or membership in the Emperor's Privy Council, which by now had usurped judicial powers from the Senate. Jurists like Papinian, Paul, and Ulpian, as heads of the Privy Council, were in effect Chief Justices, in a position to translate their enlightened philosophy into official legislation and supreme judicial decisions, to the benefit of the lower classes and the law as a whole. As despotism advanced, they extended, or at least reasserted, the claims of benevolence, of government with a conscience.

Codifying the Law. The jurist Julius Paulus alone produced 320 treatises; he and Ulpian supplied half the contents of Justinian's *Digest.* Legal literature had become voluminous; with the rise of absolutism (*see Chapter 12*) came an endless stream of administrative enactments collected (A.D. 438) into the *Theodosian Code.* Justinian decided to codify the whole of Roman law; his *Digest* (A.D. 533) is a classified collection of rules, principles, opinions, interpretations, and comments handed down by classical jurists. It condenses 2,000 books of law (3,000,000 lines) into a manageable 150,000 lines, sometimes obscuring in the process the history and motivation of great areas of Roman law. Even so, civilization owes Justinian's compiler Tribonian an immeasurable debt. But for his compendium, Rome's unwieldy bulk of legal literature would be lost. Justinian's elementary textbook, the *Institutes,* has introduced generations of students to Roman law, and is still standard. It is based largely on Gaius' classical arrangement, by Persons, Things, and Actions. (*See Readings No. 11j, k, l.*) Justinian's *Code* is possibly the ancient world's richest legacy to modern times. It forms the core of the law of continental Europe, Scotland, Quebec, and Louisiana. Through it, old Roman sagacity still guides modern society.

Roman Law and the Common Law. Even our own Anglo-Saxon common law owes much, historically and substantively, to Roman law, to which in logic, if not in solicitude for the underdog, many judge it inferior. For Roman law judges individual cases on rock-bottom rational principles, while common law looks back to precedent, which is many-faced, discordant, frequently confused, even contradictory. Modern international law is based on the Roman; the United States Supreme Court has been known, in default of any common-law precedent or Federal statute, to go to Roman law for guidance in interstate legislation.

Canon Law. When Justinian issued his code, the Empire had been Christian for over two centuries. Roman jurisprudence became the foundation of the Christian legal system. To enlightened churchmen, Roman law was a kind of progressive revelation: the civil law of the Early and Middle Republic had been smelted in the crucible of the law of nations, further refined by natural law, and Christianity came to correct whatever flaws remained. The Christian Empire embraced the pagan Empire's law with filial devotion: ecclesiastical or canon law imitates Roman law in its inner spirit and in thousands of its provisions, especially on marriage, legitimacy, inheritance, and church administration. Justinian prefaced his edition of the *Corpus of Civil Law* with the words, "In the name of our Lord Jesus Christ." (*See Reading No. 11m.*) No higher endorsement could be given to pagan legal wisdom than the seal of Christian approval.

— 12 —

THE ROAD TO ABSOLUTISM

The Roots of Absolutism. Already by 509 B.C. Rome had had enough of kings. "King" remained a hate-word throughout the Republic, and pretensions to monarchy were among the reasons alleged for Julius Caesar's murder. The idea that the consuls represent the monarchical element in the Roman constitution comes from a Greek, Polybius. When monarchy returns to Rome with Augustus, its philosophical justification is Greek. Monarchies were the prevailing governments in the Greek East in the Hellenistic Age, and prevailing governments can always find philosophers to give them a sound theoretical basis and a high moral tone. (*See Reading No. 12a.*) Ecphantus' notion of the king as created by God in His own image, made to order for Hellenistic monarchy, fits also one aspect of the Roman emperor as his subjects in the Greek East saw him: the benevolent despot. The idea of the monarch ruling on earth as God rules in heaven is the one Cicero uses to justify the *princeps'* position in the New Conservatism; Augustus was to find it useful. When the Romans succeeded the Hellenistic monarchs, a justification for kingship was waiting in the East for whichever Roman nabob proved strong enough to establish one-man rule. Brutus and Cassius murdered Caesar, but Augustus was luckier; he ruled for fifty-seven years, and was one of the few Roman emperors to die in bed.

Augustus as First Citizen. In theory, Augustus reestablished the Republic, and so the Empire continued to have consuls, puppets though they were, even under the most absolute autocrats. In practice, Augustus was a constitutional monarch, with broad civil and military powers. A subservient Senate packed with his appointees gave him (27 B.C.) proconsular authority (which made him supreme in the key provinces) and the tribunician power (whose veto gave him effective control of all legislation). Thus he combined in himself the powers formerly derived by a Marius from his personal army or by a Gracchus from his strategic position as champion of the people. Simultaneously, the Senate pressed upon him the title "Augustus," which he accepted with a pretty show of reluctance. The title implies authority, derived from increasing (*augere*) something; e.g., the bounds of empire. Efficient use of directive intelligence made this increase possible; hence Augustus is *princeps,* first citizen, partner of the Senate, father of his country. Provincial civilians took the oath of allegiance to him (*see Reading No. 12b*) as though they were soldiers; these oaths were exacted by each succeeding emperor, with growing bombast to match growing despotism. This fine Republican façade, masking an ever more absolute monarchy, is one of the most fascinating and characteristic creations of the Roman mind. Augustus' reign was a skillfully executed "program of national aggression," robbing the opposition of adherents, troops, platform, catchwords, and saints (the heroes of the early Republic); conciliating plebs, veterans, parvenus, knights, and country squires; and so consolidating the power which he passed to his enigmatic stepson Tiberius.

Tiberius and Treason. Another step on the road to absolutism was taken under Tiberius. He had a morbid, perhaps a paranoid fear of assassination, credited reports of subversion brought to him by informers (*see Reading No. 12c*), and allowed executions for treason instead of the normal sentence of exile. Treason was ill-defined; informers were rewarded from the confiscated property of their victims. The result was a reign of terror, described in some of Tacitus' most gloomily brilliant pages. The description fits later reigns and later ages: irresponsible, unchecked allegations, *agents provocateurs,* freedom of speech denied, books burned, careers ruined, the innocent driven to suicide. But only stupid men believe that tyranny now can erase the record of history hereafter. Under

Tiberius also, elections were transferred from the people to the Senate.

Of Tiberius' successors, Caligula was unhinged, and Nero appears in the pages of Tacitus as a type, the type of the tyrant. Civil war followed Nero's suicide. The winner, Vespasian, founded a new dynasty. An inscription granting him imperial powers shows that by his time the emperor regularly concluded treaties, ran the Senate, had his nominees—sometimes only one to an office—automatically elected, and in general enjoyed a free hand "to do whatever he deems best to serve the public interest." This is another milestone on the road to absolutism.

Compulsory Public Service. Emperors came to hold municipal councillors responsible for local tax collection and to exact large contributions from office-holders. This naturally made public service unpopular, and local dignitaries sought to escape from it into the army, the imperial civil service, and, in the fourth century A.D., the Christian priesthood. Emperors consequently found themselves forced to compel public service, and another step toward absolutism was taken. The papyrus from Egypt containing a Roman governor's ruling on this subject (*see Reading No. 12d*) dates from the tyrannical reign of the third and last of the Flavian dynasty, Domitian. It is noteworthy that there is no longer any question of election to these offices: the holders are appointees. The property qualification is the emperor's insurance that the nominee has enough money to make good on defaulters' taxes; the general aim was to make private citizens do public tax-collecting. If the nominees proved insolvent, the nominator was bound to take over the office himself. Trajan was a good emperor; but the letters with which his governor of Bithynia, Pliny the Younger, taxed his patience show how absolutely a less scrupulous prince might control a province. Pliny addresses his sovereign as *Dominus* (Lord), the slave's word for his master. Under Trajan it was a courtesy title; later it meant what it implied. Pliny refers to his master, besides the question of exacting contributions from municipal councillors, questions on aqueducts, baths, theaters, canals, and even on establishing a fire department (permission refused, for fear of subversive activity within the proposed firemen's guild).

Restrictions on Associations. Since Republican times, Roman law had prohibited secret societies, for fear of revolutionary plots among the lower classes. In 186 B.C. the Senate used armed force to stamp out the worship of Bacchus by secret societies. The conspiracy of Catiline was hatched by a secret society meeting in the back room of a Roman shop; Caesar's ward boss, the notorious Clodius, Lesbia's brother, took advantage of a temporary lifting of the ban to organize secret societies among the *populares* for fomenting riot. Augustus was responsible for the final lowering of the boom.

Harmless mutual-benefit burial societies were permitted. (*See Reading No. 12e.*) The bylaws of one of them make interesting reading. An amphora of good wine is part of the initiation fee; a slave member obtaining his freedom is expected to baptize the occasion similarly; members are fined for using abusive language at society dinners (menu: bread, wine, and four sardines). Even these innocuous clubs were not permitted without government licence, so fearful were even good emperors of clandestine political activity among the masses who had been denied any share in active political life. The humble officers of burial societies gave themselves titles imitating those of municipal magistrates and councillors. The charge of illicit association was one of the sticks used to beat the Christians with. (*See Chapter 13.*)

Military Anarchy. Five good emperors, Nerva, Trajan, Hadrian, Antoninus Pius, and Marcus Aurelius, made the years A.D. 96-192 happy ones. But the reign of Marcus' son Commodus was catastrophic, and the Severan dynasty that followed was alien to Roman tradition, spoke Latin with a Punic accent, and ruthlessly stamped out opposition, confiscating estates and relying heavily on army support. The murder of the last of the Severans (A.D. 235) ushered in a disastrous half-century, in which the army made and unmade nineteen emperors, and plague and inflation raged unchecked. Maximinus (*see Reading No. 12f*) was perhaps better than most. He was a peasant risen from the ranks, who had overstrained his treasury by doubling the army's pay. He confiscated private fortunes and bankrupted cities in his search for funds. Herodian's account is biased in favor of the Senate, which in A.D. 238 declared Maximinus a public enemy. He marched on Rome but was killed by his own troops. The Praetorian Guard assassinated the two emperors nominated by the Senate to succeed him.

And so it went, barbarous, extravagant, autocratic. Rome celebrated her thousandth birthday lavishly, with the son of an Arab sheik on the throne. In fear of the barbarians, Aurelian girt Rome with a twelve-mile wall. But the danger was within: Aurelian's own officers murdered him. Clearly civil and military powers needed to be separated. The strong man who undertook the reform was Diocletian.

Diocletian and the Dominate. With Diocletian the Empire became an absolute monarchy, symbolized by requiring courtiers to prostrate themselves in Oriental fashion before the monarch. Diocletian himself never saw Rome before A.D. 303; his capital was at Nicomedia in Bithynia. His reforms, so tendentiously described by the Christian Lactantius (*see Reading No. 12g*) were massive, uniform, and paternalistic. Provinces, previously forty-two in number, were broken into 109, requiring a proportionally larger bureaucracy, rising from the 109 provincial governors through twelve Vicars and four Prefects to the two Caesars and the two Augusti, now addressed with titles more grandiloquent than ever. Besides persecuting Christians, Diocletian debased the currency and then tried to curb the resulting inflation by putting ceilings on wages and prices (A.D. 301; *see Reading No. 12h*), in an edict whose detailed provisions make it the most valuable surviving ancient economic document. Given the Empire's unity, a planned economy might have worked, but Diocletian's scheme was too rigid, neither distinguishing between wholesale and retail prices nor allowing for seasonal price and wage shifts. Furthermore, it attacked the problem at the wrong end, trying to deal with the results of inflation instead of its causes. It failed, but it is typical of Diocletian's totalitarianism. Ironically, the Dominate destroyed the prosperity of the very propertied class which had accepted it in the narrow-minded pursuit of self-interest.

Absolute Monarchy. Diocletian's successor, who consolidated absolutism, was Constantine the Great. His son Constantius' sense of his own importance is graphically described in the account of his triumphant entry into Rome (*see Reading No. 12i*) by Ammianus Marcellinus, Rome's greatest historian since Tacitus. From his pages Constantius emerges as a cruel bureaucrat, head of a spy-ridden police state. Constantius is Ammianus' villain; his hero is Julian the Apostate, the last of the pagans, who turned the power of the absolutist state against the Christians. He tried to organize the pagan clergy in imitation of the Christian hierarchy, wrote vigorously against the Christians, excluded them from public employment, taxed them excessively, and condoned persecution. Wounded in battle, he died like Socrates, conversing with philosophers on immortality. Christianity lived on; its trials and triumph form the subject of the next chapter.

As we take leave of pagan Rome, in which by now classes and masses alike were under absolutist sway, let us resolve some contradictions by re-emphasizing that in the Empire's prosperous days it was the propertied classes who collaborated with the régime, profited from it, and sang the praises of the Roman peace. The masses, in general, were politically ignorant and apathetic, strictly regimented, grievously exploited, and only superficially Romanized. It was to be among them that the Christian message of equality in God's sight and happiness at last in Heaven was to be most enthusiastically received.

ROME AND CHRISTIANITY

The Persecution under Nero. Christ's crucifixion under Tiberius must have impressed the Roman ruling-class mind only slightly; Pontius Pilate, as a retired civil servant, probably had only the vaguest recollection of the incident, and Christianity was only one of many Oriental cults to which the ruling class attached little importance. But by Nero's time (A.D. 54-68) the sect had made great headway among humble folk in Rome's Eastern provinces and even in the capital itself. Peter and Paul were probably both in Rome under Nero. The Emperor found it politic to blame the Christians for Rome's great fire of A.D. 64 (*see Reading No. 13a*), and other pretexts were not wanting for persecuting on political grounds this sect which so obstinately refused to recognize the Emperor's divinity. Christians were charged with illegal association, subversive activity and insulting imperial officials. Even Tacitus, though a reasonable and sympathetic man, accepts hearsay evidence on abominable Christian practices, confuses Christians with Jews, and apparently twists into charges of cannibalism the Christian communion, wherein bread and wine symbolize Christ's body and blood. As an imperial civil servant, he could not have failed to regard Christian refusal to worship the Empire's gods as perverse and dangerous.

The Policy under Trajan. Tacitus' friend Pliny, as governor of Bithynia early in the second century A.D., found himself in a province of great strategic importance which had early proved fertile ground for Christian proselytizing, and not only among the lower class. He inadvertently gives us evidence (*see Reading No. 13b*) of widespread decline of the pagan cult: temples deserted, holy days ignored, sacrifices neglected. Pliny is a humane man, and Trajan a righteous prince, but neither of them can see any sense in Christianity, and both regard it as actively pernicious. But both, though Trajan rather more than Pliny, show that respect for due process which is one of the most admirable characteristics of the Roman legal mind at work. It is heartening to read Trajan's advice against witch-hunting, and his proud rejecting of anonymous information as unworthy of the standards of his enlightened age. Trajan's attitude set the pattern in the provinces throughout the second century. Even so, persecutions beset the Church during Marcus Aurelius' otherwise benign reign.

Early Christian Worship.   Pliny's letter is also valuable as informing us about early Christian cult practices, including hymn-singing, respect for the Ten Commandments, and taking communion. The reference to deaconesses suggests that in his time the Church already had a hierarchy, and his evidence on the equality of Christian women is also interesting.

Scandalous attacks, like Tacitus', on the new creed early provoked from Christians a literature of self-defense, called apologetics, in which they stress the innocence of their worship. Justin Martyr, one of these early apologists, gives us precious information about baptism, confirmation, the kiss of peace, the observance of Sunday (*see Reading No. 13c*), Bible reading, sermons, and the practice of Christian charity. Clearly in his time the Church was still poor and humble, not yet rich or powerful enough to indulge in the pomp and ceremony which it could afford and which it was politic for it to adopt when it finally achieved imperial recognition.

The Making of the Canon.   It took the Church a long time to decide which of the scriptures read in its services were to bear the stamp of official authority. At the end of the second century A.D. the New Testament as we know it was still not formed, the four Gospels, Acts, and Paul's letters being the only parts universally recognized as canonical. About A.D. 150 a vast quantity of "apocryphal" books still circulated: other gospels (including one attributed to doubting Thomas), books approved by some congregations and not by others, sayings of Christ not found in the four Gospels, non-Pauline letters (of which *Hebrews* is a canonical example), a forged correspondence between Seneca and Paul, various visions of judgment, and the Acts of John, Peter, Andrew, Philip, and others. The original language of all these works was Greek, but they are included here because they circulated in the Roman Empire and made an impact upon the Roman mind. The Acts of John (*see Reading No. 13d*) present a valuable picture of Rome's Eastern provinces in the mid-second century, and provide typical examples of the taste, intellectual level, and ideals of uneducated early Christians. The Evangelist's preaching to the submissive bedbugs and the moral he draws from their obedience make a charming story, and one whose intellectual climate is not far from that of the Middle Ages.

The body of doctrine collected in these apocryphal books is rather eccentric than orthodox. The books were used by sects like the Gnostics and the Manichees, which were to be branded heretical or schismatic. For the early Church did not enjoy an uninterrupted love feast; it suffered fierce internal conflicts, and backslidings in the face of persecution were numerous.

Atrocities. Organized persecution of Christians was rare during the second century. The persecution in Marcus Aurelius' reign was a reaction against plague and inflation within the empire and barbarian incursions on the frontier, all of which were interpreted as meaning that the angry pagan gods were demanding sacrifices. In A.D. 177 forty-eight Christian men and women were tortured in Lyons and Vienne with the Emperor's approval. We hear of beating, rape, stoning, imprisonment, confinement in the stocks, strangling, impalement, throwing to the wild beasts, and giving the bodies to be torn by dogs or thrown into the Rhône. A set of minutes of the Roman Senate found at Italica in Spain, discussing the reduction for the upper class of the burdens imposed by spectacles in the amphitheaters (*see Reading No. 13e*) has recently been interpreted as a document illustrating this persecution. Men of property in Gaul needed a supply of cheap victims for spectacles that they were required by ancient custom to give in Lyons; it occurred to the imperial government to let the priests of the imperial cult acquire cheaply and use instead of gladiators Christian prisoners who had been condemned to death. This satisfied ancient Gallic religious custom at minimum expense to the propertied class. The Emperor needed Gallic loyalty in the face of the barbarian invasions and perhaps never foresaw that his concessions were the thin end of a pernicious wedge. The demand for victims grew apace, and powerful pressure groups found a relief for their purses in unpopular characters like the Christians, who could be condemned to death.

Organized Persecutions. The military anarchy of the third century brought with it frustrations, worked out on the Christians, who by this time had become a powerful state within the state. Under Decius (249-251) a loyalty oath was required; under Valerian, who had suffered severe military reverses in 257, an organized effort was made to murder Church leaders and impose economic sanctions upon Christian property-holders. One of the victims of Valerian's prosecution, Cyprian, Bishop of Carthage, has left a letter (*see Reading No. 13f*) vividly recording the feelings of his flock as they awaited the death sentence, and the heroism, even eagerness, of those who were to suffer martyrdom for Christ. This persecution lasted from 259 to 270. The last, under Diocletian, was even more severe, and raged from 303 to 311. Churches were raided at dawn, the priests mocked, the bishops forced to offer pagan sacrifice, the scriptures burned, the buildings razed to the ground. Christians were deprived of due process, degraded in rank, enslaved, stripped, scourged, tortured on the gridiron, burned alive, and falsely accused of responsibility for a fire in the palace. Finally, Diocletian's colleague Galerius, conscience-striken on his deathbed, issued an Edict of Toleration (311) which legalized Christianity and prepared the way for its final triumph.

The "Edict of Milan." Constantine was pro-Christian, his colleague Licinius pro-pagan. Their compromise at Milan (A.D. 313; *see Reading No. 13g*) guaranteed complete freedom of worship to pagans and Christians alike. The translation, heavily cut, does not reproduce the almost intolerable "Federal prose" of the original, which is in Greek, being a directive to governors of the

Eastern provinces. This verbiage is apparently an in-separable adjunct of bureaucracy, but it is a far cry from old Cato's rugged style. Later legislation exempted clerics from compulsory public services (*see Reading No. 13h*), repealed Augustus' laws against celibacy, made Sunday a holiday, authorized the freeing of slaves by declaration in churches, and allowed the Church to receive legacies and try cases in ecclesiastical courts. Pagan domestic sacrifices were expressly forbidden; it was now pagan and not Christian private associations which were dangerous to the régime. Public pagan services were not prohibited, being regarded as harmlessly old-fashioned. Portents like the striking of a public building by lightning still, as late as 321, occasioned the consulting of soothsayers. And the abortive revival under Julian the Apostate (360-363) proves that paganism still had vitality.

The Triumph of Christianity. Pagan worship was not abolished, nor pagan temples systematically destroyed, until near the end of Theodosius' reign (392). In the late fourth century the chief intellectual lights of the Roman world were learned and powerful bishops like Ambrose of Milan and Augustine of Hippo. When Ambrose made Theodosius do public penance for atrocities committed in the amphitheater at Thessalonica (390), it foreshadowed medieval conflicts between Pope and Emperor. Christianity as the state religion tempted its hierarchy to political ambitions and to attempts at increasing its power by heresy-hunting. (*See Reading No. 13i.*) The strongest heresies were the Donatist in Africa, which turned upon the question of taking back into the Church backsliders who had recanted under the pressure of the persecutions, and the Arian in the East, which offered a monotheistic solution to the problem of reconciling the unity of the Father with the divinity of the Son. The emperors intervened in the controversies in two ways, wherein the Roman mind may be said to show its double legacy: sometimes they imposed orthodoxy in the Roman way; sometimes they veered with the winds of doctrine in the Greek. By 385 the Church was executing heretics, another irony and a grim anticipation of the Middle Ages.

Christianity's triumph infused new life into the Empire,

helped to civilize the barbarians, formed the mind of the
Middle Ages, and helped preserve the classical heritage.
But imperial interventions in Church affairs, plus civil
difficulties with usurpers, and the constant barbarian
menace combined to force the fourth-century Empire
further into absolutism, and to hasten its decline and fall.
The Church, whose theology was indebted to Greek philosophy, its high standard of morality to the Roman
Republic, and its hierarchy, pomp, and ceremony to the
Roman Empire, is our final ancient example of the syn-
thesizing, creatively borrowing force of the Roman mind
at work.

EPILOGUE

ROME AND AMERICA

We leave Rome as Christianity is triumphing, and the
barbarian hammering at the gates, and turn in conclusion
to some striking likenesses between Rome and America,
and some equally striking differences, the latter centering,
let us hope, in the attitudes toward the use of violence
and in the opportunities offered to the common man.

The Roman and American Republics. First, four
respects in which the Roman Republic resembled the
American.

1. *The Use of Leisure.* Romans of Plautus' time (about
251-184 B.C.) could occupy their leisure with festivals,
in the atmosphere of an American state fair, noisy, rol-
licking, full of gaiety and wine-bibbing. By 80 B.C. Pom-
peii boasted a stone amphitheater with *graffiti* scratched
on its walls proving that Pompeian girls sighed for favorite gladiators like modern Americans for film stars.
The point of comparison is the fondness of both Romans
and Americans for spectator sports. While no American
pastimes are as lethal as gladiatorial shows, there is
perhaps scope for the satirist's pen in the spectacle of a
modern football crowd bound for the stadium on an Oc-
tober Saturday afternoon.

2. *Imitation and Originality.* We have stated the case
for Roman borrowing as creative and made it good by
examples from Plautine comedy, Vergilian pastoral, and

Catullan and Propertian love poetry. But as we consider
the analogy with America, we must in candor record
that Terence was more derivative than Plautus, that Roman pastoral includes its quota of rather lifeless shepherds and shepherdesses, and that Roman love poetry
comes to an early end. As to American literature, as
late as the mid-nineteenth century, an Englishman could
ask, "Who reads an American book?" And, indeed, early
American literature has its share of derivative sermons,
poems, and novels. Yet American literature before 1850
has its admirers, more numerous abroad than at home,
as witness the French fondness for Poe or Cooper. As
Roman literature came to stand firmly on its own feet at
the end of the Republic with Cicero's speeches or Vergil's
poems, so America, after about 1850, could point to
Bryan's golden oratory or Whitman's epic love for the
American land.

3. *Materialism.* In ideas and in things, Romans and
Americans share a love for the practical. (This may ex-
plain the early death of Roman love poetry and the slim
sales of poetry in America.) Rome's greatest philosopher
was a materialist, Lucretius, for whom philosophy was
no academic subject but could mean freedom from fear.
So America's great contribution to philosophy is the
pragmatism of a James or a Dewey, whose analogy with
Rome is not less striking when we recall that James called
pragmatism "a new name for some old ways of thinking."
In the domain of practical life, the Roman competence
at engineering is like the American, and Roman aqueducts, roads, and plumbing have their American counterparts.

4. *Conservatism.* In the area of politics, the analogy
between Roman and American conservatives, however
little known to the latter, seems closer now than it did
twenty years ago, though even the New Deal was conservative in the sense that it sought to prop up the cap-
italist system rather than to undermine it. Roman conservatives made land grants, American ones passed
Homestead Acts. And the farther back one goes in
American history, the closer the analogy becomes, until
the Federalists seem like Ciceros in wigs and breeches.
Liberals like Jefferson, too, drew inspiration from Rome,

in architecture and in fostering education as well as in Tacitean criticism of the *status quo*.

The Roman and American Empires. Some journalists speak, somewhat chauvinistically, of ours as "the American Century." It is certainly a century in which America has had to assume responsibilities not unlike those of the Roman Empire. Here, however, differences will loom larger than likenesses, as four examples will show.

1. *Liberty and Security.* Here we tread on delicate ground. A record of higher regard for the underdog, better mass education, and a greater reluctance to resort to violence has made the American sacrifice of liberty to security far less complete than the Roman. When Roman provincials swore an oath to Augustus, called Septimius Severus "most divine among emperors that have ever been," or prostrated themselves before Diocletian, they had explored the road to absolutism much farther than Americans have ever done. But some observers see dangers to liberty in close alliance between politics and either big business or organized labor; in an alleged "one-party press"; in the failure of American troops in World War II to be articulate about what they were fighting for; in popular apathy in the face of assaults upon due process or minority rights; and the electorate is charged with putting desire for security ahead of the search for competence when votes are cast. Others regard these fears as exaggerated, deny that liberty has been infringed, and regard the present government as the apotheosis of "the American way." While we await history's verdict, it will do no harm to recall that eternal vigilance is the price of liberty.

2. *Anti-intellectualism.* American analogies might be found for the decline of literature under the Roman Empire, the book-burning and irresponsible character assassination on grounds of subversion under Tiberius, the neglect of intellectuals complained of by Juvenal, and the widespread, irrational belief in astrology and magic charms. Indeed, some observers detect a growing anti-intellectualism in American life, evidenced, they claim, by a spirit of conformity in contemporary literature and journalism, bigotry and witch-hunting on the part of

Senatorial investigating committees, the low esteem of painters, sculptors, and poets, and even the sale of printed horoscopes in drugstores, and the vogue of eccentric or revivalist religious cults. But these analogies seem far fetched. Novelists like Saul Bellow give grounds for hope that ours is no literary Silver Age; the Senate has repudiated the excesses of its own committees, creative artists find a ready market for their work, museums are crowded, and television acquaints the public with modern art; while charges of superstition seem exaggerated. But intellectuals tend to be snobbish; the very mass education vital to democracy may produce and encourage mediocrity; and insecurity over social status or worry over world unrest may bring out abnormal streaks of intolerance. In short, anti-intellectualism is a clear and present danger, against which Rome's experience may serve as warning.

3. *Supremacy in Architecture.* The Roman Empire was supreme in architecture, especially in ambitious, axially symmetrical plans like that evolved by the Greek Apollodorus of Damascus for Trajan's Forum, or in the Spaniard Hadrian's daring use of concrete, or in the native Roman genius of Domitian's architect Rabirius. Roman public and private wealth gave scope to the talent of foreign and native architects alike, and the result has never been surpassed in grandeur of effect or daring of plan until the days of the skyscraper. So, nowadays, American government and business have subsidized to good effect the genius of a whole generation of brilliant architects, foreign, naturalized, and native: the German Gropius, the Finn Saarinen, the American Frank Lloyd Wright.

4. *One World.* We have not glossed over the Roman Empire's defects: bureaucracy, corruption, persecution of minorities, absolutism; analogies for them might not be difficult to find in America or elsewhere in the modern world. But there were virtues, too, and if American analogies to them are hard to find the loss is ours: generous granting of citizenship, no race discrimination, long, world-wide peace and security, and the guarantee to all of the due process of law. The Roman Empire was One World. Many modern men of good will want world unity;

they may draw salutary lessons from the Roman experience, which proves that unity is no guarantee of liberty. Yet liberty may degenerate into the unbridled licence of nations fighting useless wars. Rome found that survival required sacrifices, sometimes of a kind intolerable to modern liberals. In our experiment with the United Nations, we must determine what sacrifices are necessary, safeguarding the essentials: freedom of speech and of conscience, freedom from want and from fear. At moments in her history, Rome provided some of these; toward the end, she denied them all. The granting and the denial were both the result of the Roman mind at work for good and for ill. An examination of the result of that working can teach us what, with directive intelligence, to borrow (creatively), and what to avoid.

Part II

SELECTED READINGS FROM LATIN AND GREEK SOURCES

— Reading No. 1 —

ROMANS ON THEIR ORIGINS

Eutropius (flourished A.D. *363) published his* Digest of Roman History *some eleven centuries after the traditional date of Rome's founding. But its basis is an earlier digest, of Livy's 142-book history,* From the Founding of the City, *the original written 29* B.C.-A.D. *11. Cicero published* On the Republic *in 54* B.C.; *no extant connected account of Rome's beginnings is earlier than this. Thus our earliest sources date from seven hundred years after the events they describe.*

✓   ✓   ✓

a. EUTROPIUS: *Digest of Roman History,* I, 1-4

The Roman Empire, virtually the humblest in its origins, the greatest in its world-wide expansion, that human memory can recall, began with Romulus, son of Rhea Silvia, a Vestal Virgin, and, allegedly, of Mars. He and his brother Remus were twins. He grew up among shepherds, as a highwayman; at eighteen he founded a primitive city on the Palatine Hill, on April 21, in the third year of the Sixth Olympiad; 394 years—striking an average between upper and lower traditional dates—after the fall of Troy [753 B.C.].

Once the city was founded—called Rome after him— he granted citizenship to a host of his neighbors, and chose one hundred elders, called Senators, whose advice he followed in everything. Then, since he and his people had no wives, he invited the tribes nearest Rome to a festival, and carried off their daughters. The injustice of this act moved the tribes to war, but he beat them. . . .

When after a sudden storm he disappeared, in the thirty-seventh year of his reign, he was believed to have ascended into heaven, and was deified. For a year thereafter the Senators ruled Rome, five days each.

Then Numa Pompilius was made king. Though he waged not a single war, he profited the state no less than Romulus, for he laid down laws and customs for the Romans. Before his reign they had been so used to battles that they were considered half-savage highwaymen. He divided the year into ten months; up to then it had been confused and unregulated. And he founded at Rome an infinite series of religious rites and temples.

His successor was Tullus Hostilius. He took up war again, beat the men of Alba, Veii, and Fidenae, situated respectively twelve, six and eighteen miles from Rome, and enlarged the city by adding to it the Caelian Hill. After a thirty-two year reign, he and his family were struck by lightning and burned to death.

———

b. LIVY: *Epitome,* 1b

[Ancus Marcius] beat the Latins, distributed lots of land on the Aventine Hill, extended Rome's borders, and planted a colony at Ostia. He revived the rites Numa had founded. To test the skill of Attus Navius, the augur, he asked him, it is said, whether what he was thinking of could be done; when Attus said it could, Ancus bade him cut a whetstone in two with a razor, which Attus promptly did.

Ancus reigned twenty-four years. In his reign Lucumo, son of Demaratus of Corinth, came to Rome from the Etruscan city of Tarquinia. Ancus befriended him; he began to call himself Tarquinius Priscus and succeeded Ancus as king. He increased the Senate to two hundred, subdued the Latins, held races in the Circus, increased the cavalry squadrons, built a wall around the city, and dug sewers. Ancus' children murdered him when he had reigned thirty-eight years.

His successor was Servius Tullius, son of Corniculana, a noblewomen who became a prisoner-of-war. While he was still a child in his cradle, a halo was seen round his head. He held the first census . . . [a population of

80,000 is recorded], extended Rome's city boundaries, added the Quirinal, Viminal, and Esquiline Hills to the city, and built on the Aventine, jointly with the Latins, a temple to Diana. After a reign of forty-four years he was killed by Tarquinius Priscus' son Lucius, at the instigation of his own daughter Tullia.

Next Lucius Tarquinius, the Proud, against the will of both senate and people, usurped the throne. He kept an armed bodyguard about him. From the spoils of his war with the Volscians he built a temple to Jupiter on the Capitoline Hill. He tricked Gabii into submission. His sons went to Delphi and asked the oracle which of them would rule at Rome. They were told that the first to kiss his mother would rule. The sons misunderstood the oracle, but Junius Brutus, who had gone with them, pretended to stumble, and kissed the earth. The event proved his interpretation correct, for Tarquin the Proud was acting so highhandedly that everyone hated him. To cap the climax, his son Sextus one night raped Lucretia. She summoned her father Tricipitinus and her husband Collatinus, made them swear to avenge her death, and stabbed herself. The result was the expulsion of Tarquin —chiefly Brutus' doing—after a twenty-five-year reign. Then the first consuls were elected, Lucius Junius Brutus and Lucius Tarquinius Collatinus.

---

c. CICERO: *On the Republic,* II, 2, 4, and 45-48

[Cato the Elder] used to say that our state was better than others because elsewhere individuals had given laws and institutions to their commonwealths . . . , whereas ours had been established not by one brain but by many, not in one man's lifetime, but over several generations and centuries.

"Does any civilized commonwealth," said Scipio, "have as brilliant and far famed an origin as our city, founded by Romulus? His father was Mars. (Let us follow the familiar tradition, wisely established by our forefathers, that divine descent as well as divine intelligence should be ascribed to distinguished historical figures.) By order of

Amulius, king of Alba, who feared for his throne, the new-born infant, so the story goes, with his brother Remus, was left to die on the Tiber bank, where a wild beast suckled him, shepherds found him and reared him in their simple hard-working ways. He grew up, legend says, so extraordinarily strong and fierce-spirited that he won the willing allegiance of all the farmers who lived where Rome now stands. Now we come from fable to fact: he volunteered to lead them, sacked Alba Longa, a mighty stronghold for those days, and killed King Amulius."

———

King Tarquin, stained as he was with the blood of the best of kings, was unbalanced, and in his fear of paying the supreme penalty for his crime, wanted to inspire fear in others. Besides, the spoils of successful war made him arrogant: his own conduct and his family's lust were equally uninhibited. So when his eldest son raped the chaste and noble Lucretia . . . and that highhanded act drove . . . her to suicide, Lucius Brutus, a hero as wise as he was brave, struck from his countryman's necks the galling yoke of slavery. Though he was not responsible for the government, he defended the common interest and set the precedent for the Roman attitude that where civil liberty is at stake no one is irresponsible. He took the initiative in rousing the whole citizenry to a decree of exile against Tarquin, his sons and his whole clan, based on the latest charges of outrage, lodged by Lucretia's father and her next of kin, and on the Tarquins' long record of arrogance and injustice. Do you see, then, how a king turned overlord and a basic flaw in one man turned a good commonwealth into the worst type of all? This overlord the Greeks call a tyrant, defining a king as one who takes a fatherly interest in his people and preserves for his subjects an excellent way of life. Good as this type of government is, it is especially liable to degenerate completely, for the king who turns into an overlord, above the law, automatically becomes a tyrant, the foulest and most sinister, accursed, loathsome creature imaginable; he only looks like a man: even the hugest of wild beasts cannot rival his monstrous cruelty. For how can you properly apply the name of man to one who recognizes no common bond of law between himself and his fellow-citizens, no link of shared culture between himself and all mankind?

---

d. LIVY: *From the Founding of the City,* Preface, 6-11

Rome's foundation legends, which are epic poetry rather than sound factual documents, I intend neither to affirm nor to deny. Tales of ancient times have the special privilege of ennobling the origins of cities by mingling the human with the divine, and if any people has the right to deify its beginnings and make the gods responsible for them, the Roman people are so famous in war that when they claim Mars as their founder's father and their own, the nations of the earth should acquiesce as gracefully as they acquiesce in Roman rule.

But this, I feel, is of no great consequence; rather let my reader concentrate hard upon the way of life, the individual heroes and the civil and military techniques by which the Empire was won and expanded. Then let him follow with his mind's eye the gradual relaxing of discipline, the decadence, rapid decline, and headlong fall of morals, down to our own time, in which we find our ills and our panaceas equally unendurable.

The saving grace, the special reward of the study of history is that you survey a variety of object-lessons set forth as in a monumental relief, from which you may choose for yourself and your country what to imitate and what to avoid.

---

e. LIVY: *From the Founding of the City,* VIII, 40

Among conflicting facts and authorities choice is difficult. The record has, I think, been falsified by funeral eulogies and deceptive inscriptions under portraits, as individual families, deliberately lying, monopolize the credit for military and civil honors, which unquestionably confuses our records of individual exploits and public events. And no reliable historian contemporary with those ancient times survives.

— Reading No. 2 —

CLASS STRUGGLE

*The selections, ranging in dramatic date from 494 B.C.
to A.D. 322, include a parable on many members and
one body; two descriptions of the plight of the landless
before the Gracchan reforms [133 B.C.]; an account of
the slave uprisings of 73-71 B.C.; advice to Caesar on
ending the class struggle; Augustus on his benefactions to
the plebs; a satire on a self-made man; a vignette of the
life of the poor in the noisy jungle of imperial Rome; a
Stoic view of slavery; an account of a bread riot in Asia
Minor [early second century A.D.]; and a legal provision
for assistance to poor children in Africa. The total impression is one of extremes of wealth and poverty, occasionally alleviated by reformer's zeal, private philanthropy, or imperial benevolence.*

✦   ✦   ✦

a. LIVY: *From the Founding of the City,* II, 32

Once upon a time, before the human body had become
co-ordinated, each of its members had its own ideas and
its own voice. The other members were angry because
everything they did profited the belly, while the belly, idle
at the centre of things, did nothing but enjoy the proffered
dainties. So the members decided to go on strike: the
hands would bring the mouth no food, the mouth would
accept none, the teeth would do no chewing. While in
their spite their intent was to starve the belly into subjec-
tion, the members themselves and the whole body wasted
away to nothing. This proved that the belly, too, had not
been an idle member, that it provided as well as took
nourishment, sending into the bloodstream and all over

the body an equal share of the digested food which gives us life and strength.

---

b. APPIAN: *Civil Wars*, I, 1, 7

The rich seized most of the unallotted public lands, and growing ever more confident that no one would ever take it away from them, began to grab neighboring plots and the few acres of the poor, sometimes by persuasion and purchase, sometimes by force, so that eventually they farmed vast plantations instead of individual properties, using slaves as farmhands and shepherds, for fear that free laborers would be drafted into the army. Their slave-owning was very profitable, for the slaves were prolific, and, not being liable for military duty, were free to multiply. Thus the nabobs grew extremely rich, and Italy was full of slaves, while free Italian manpower decreased, ground down by poverty, taxes, and conscription.

---

c. PLUTARCH: *Life of Tiberius Gracchus*, 9

Tiberius Gracchus . . . would stand on the Rostra and plead for the poor: "The nomad wild beasts of Italy have each a den or lair to lie in, but those who fight and die for Italy get their share of air and light, and nothing more; without homes, without roots, men with families live like vagrants. . . . They fight and die that others may live in wealth and luxury, while they, the so-called 'lords of the earth' have not a single lump of clay to call their own."

---

d. APPIAN: *Civil Wars*, I, 14, 116-120

The Thracian Spartacus, an ex-Roman soldier who had been taken prisoner and sold as a gladiator to the training school at Capua, persuaded about seventy men to risk their lives for freedom rather than for spectators' amusement. They overpowered the guards, robbed travellers to arm themselves with clubs and daggers, and ran away to a hideout on Mt. Vesuvius, where many runaway slaves and a few free farmhands joined their outlaw band. . . . Spartacus soon had an army of 70,000 men. . . .

[For three years he consistently beat the Roman armies, until in a final battle] he suffered a spear wound in the thigh, fell on one knee, held his shield before him, and fought on until he and the bulk of his comrades were surrounded and killed. The rest of his army was thrown into disorder and butchered wholesale. The casualties were too many to count, and Spartacus' body was never found. . . . The remnant of his army, . . . six thousand men, was captured and crucified along the whole Appian Way from Capua to Rome.

---

e. [SALLUST]: *To Caesar on the Commonwealth*, II, 5-6

I accept the tradition of a bipartite state, patrician and plebeian. Since the plebeian majority conflicted with patrician authority, the state suffered frequent secessions, which steadily decreased patrician power and increased plebeian rights. The plebs was free to secede because no one's power was above the law: whatever precedence a noble had over a common man was based on good repute and heroism, not on wealth or arrogance. . . . But when unemployment and poverty gradually drove plebeians from their farms into vagrancy, they began to covet other people's property, and to put their liberty and their country up for sale . . . [until by now] they are quite unfit for citizenship. . . . But I have high hopes that an injection of new citizens will wake them all up to the blessings of liberty. . . . I advise you to mix new citizens with old and set them up in colonies. This will produce a stronger army and a lower class kept from subversive activity by good jobs.

Of course I foresee how the nobles will rant and rage at this. How they will bluster, crying, "The world is turned upside-down!" "This makes citizens into slaves!" "This will turn our free commonwealth into a totalitarian state!" "Dictatorship!" "Handouts to a rabble!"

---

f. AUGUSTUS: *Autobiography*, 15

Disbursement to the Roman plebs: by my father's will, 300 sesterces each [44 B.C.]. From war booty, 400 sesterces each [29 B.C.]. From my own estate, 400 sesterces each [23 B.C.]. Bought out of my own pocket, twelve doles of grain. A third outright gift, 400 sesterces each [12 B.C.]. Minimum number of beneficiaries each time: 250,000.

———

g. PETRONIUS: *Trimalchio's Banquet,* 75-77 (abridged)

[*A self-made man speaks.*] Once I was just like you; ability has put me where I am today, just bursting with prosperity. It's my saving ways that have made me a millionaire. When I came from Asia, I was no bigger than that candlestick. For fourteen years I was my master's favorite, and, not to brag, my mistress's, too. With Heaven's help I got to run the place, tricked my master into remembering me in his will, and inherited a senatorial fortune. But no one's ever satisfied, and I wanted to get into business. I built five freighters, loaded them with wine—worth a fortune then—and shipped it to Rome. You'd have thought I planned it that way: every ship sank; 30,000,000 sesterces down Neptune's gullet in a day. Did I grow fainthearted? No; I built more, bigger, luckier ships. And my wife did the right thing: sold her jewels and clothes and gave me the take: 100 gold pieces. That put my pot on the boil. By Heaven's will, in one quick voyage, I made a fat 10,000,000. Right away I paid off the mortgage, built a town house, cornered the slave and cattle market; whatever I touched grew like a honeycomb. When I was richer than my whole home town, I retired, and began friendly finance to freedmen. I built this mansion. It used to be a hovel; now it's a regular temple: twenty bedrooms, two porticos (marble veneer), upstairs wine cellar, master bedroom, sitting-room for the ball-and-chain, a fine porter's lodge, and plenty of guestrooms.

———

h. JUVENAL: *Satire* III (Selection from Dryden's translation, 1693)

What house secure from noise the poor can keep
When ev'n the rich can scarce afford to sleep?
So dear it costs to purchase rest in Rome.

And hence the sources of diseases come.
The drover who his fellow-drover meets
In narrow passages of winding streets:
The wagoners, that curse their standing teams
Would wake ev'n drowsy Drusus from his dreams.
And yet the wealthy will not brook delay;
But sweep above our heads, and make their way;
In lofty litters borne, and read and write,
Or sleep at ease: the shutters make it night.

---

i. SENECA: *Moral Epistles*, XLVII, 10-11

Remember, please, that your so-called slave is a man
like you, enjoying the same sunshine, breathing, living,
mortal like you! Your social positions might so easily
be reversed! In Marius' revolution [roughly 104-86 B.C.]
luck deserted many a scion of the highest nobility; they
expected their military service to bring them to high
places, but some found themselves reduced to herding
sheep, others to a squatter's life in a country hovel. Can
you afford to scorn a man whose servile lot may befall
you even while you are scorning him? I have no wish to
involve myself in large questions and discuss our treatment of slaves, which is to the highest degree overweening,
sadistic, and insulting. In brief, my advice is: treat your
inferiors as you would wish your superiors to treat you.
Whenever it occurs to you that you can do as you like
with your slave, remember that your master can do as he
likes with you. "But," you say, "I have no master." There
is a long life before you: you may yet have one.

---

j. PHILOSTRATUS: *Life of Apollonius of Tyana*, I, 15

When Apollonius got to Aspendus, . . . there was
nothing for sale but cattle fodder and starvation rations,
for the rich had cornered the grain for export. Old and
young, furious with the governor, had lit a fire to burn
him alive, though he had fallen at the feet of the Emper-
or's statue. . . . Apollonius turned to the crowd and sig-
naled that they should listen. They fell silent in wonder
. . . and even shifted their fire to the nearby altars. The

governor, encouraged, said, *"X* and *Y"* (naming names) "are responsible for this famine, for they have locked up the grain in their warehouses all over the province." The men of Aspendus wanted to track these plantation-owners down, but Apollonius shook his head and signed to them to get those responsible to give up the grain voluntarily. When the guilty ones arrived, he almost burst into speech against them, in his sympathy with the tears of the crowd of women and children, and with the moaning of the old men half-dead with hunger. But he kept his vow of silence and wrote his accusation on a slate which he gave to the governor to read, as follows: "Apollonius to the grain merchants of Aspendus: the earth is the mother of us all, for she is just, but you in your injustice have acted as though she were your mother exclusively. If you do not stop, I will not let you exist upon her." In terror they filled the market place with grain and the city came back to life.

---

k. *Theodosian Code,* XI, 27, 2

We have learned that provincials, under stress of poverty and famine, are selling their children or giving them as security. Therefore, whoever is found without income and having grave difficulty in supporting his children, the privy purse shall save him from ruin. Proconsuls, governors, and accounting officers in all Africa are authorized to distribute immediately emergency funds and subsistence from the state warehouses to all noted as being in dire need. For to let anyone die of hunger or be provoked thereby to crime is not the Roman way.

— Reading No. 3 —

MANIFEST DESTINY

Passages to illustrate the growth, policy, and effects of Roman imperialism: Rome's absorption of Latium [338 B.C.]; her "liberation" of Greece [196 B.C.]; how Rome delivered an ultimatum [168 B.C.]; a Jewish view [about 160 B.C.] of Rome's qualifications to rule an empire; Cicero on how to govern a province [59 B.C.]; Vergil [about 23 B.C.] on the virtues of the velvet glove and the iron hand; two comments, both by the same historian (Tacitus), one imperialist [dramatic date A.D. 70], one anti-imperialist [dramatic date A.D. 83-84]; and a panegyric of the Empire under Antonius Pius [about A.D. 150].

✓   ✓   ✓

a. LIVY: *From the Founding of the City,* VIII, 11-14 (abridged)

The Latins all surrendered, just in time to prevent the victorious consular army from burning their crops; the Campanians followed suit. Latium and Capua were punished by confiscating their lands, and dividing them among the Roman plebs, about two acres per head, more or less, depending on the distance from Rome. The Campanian upper class, which had not revolted, was given Roman citizenship, and the act commemorated on a bronze plaque in the temple of Castor at Rome. The Campanian people were ordered to pay the 1600 members of their upper class 450 *denarii* [about $90] a year each.

The Latins, infuriated at the confiscation of their property, revolted again. The Roman consuls decided to extend their strategy, making a greater and more spirited effort, from the siege of a single city to the complete domination of Latium. Inexorably, by the siege or surrender of successive cities, they subjected all Latium. After stationing occupation forces in the recaptured towns, they returned to Rome to a triumph unanimously accorded. They also received equestrian statues in the Forum, then a rare honor.

The consuls reported on each Latin people separately, and each was treated according to its deserts. The various recommendations included: full citizenship and religious rights; punishment of ringleaders only; in an exceptionally stubborn case, dismantlement of walls, deportation of senate, and Roman colonization of confiscated lands; confiscation of fleet (the punishment of Antium, which also received a colony, in which, however, Antiates might enroll; the beaks [*rostra*] of the Antiate ships were used to ornament a speakers' platform in the Roman Forum, hence called the Rostra); in general, cancellation of Latin cities' rights to intermarriage, trade, and common councils with each other.

b. LIVY: *From the Founding of the City,* XXXIII, 31-33 (abridged)

The time had come for the Isthmian games. This time an unusually large and cosmopolitan crowd had gathered, drawn not only by all the usual attractions but by curiosity about the future status and fortune of Greece. All sorts of conjectures were in the air; that the Romans would withdraw completely from Greece no one dreamed. When the spectators were seated, a herald came forward with a trumpeter, as is customary at the solemn opening of the games, and when silence had fallen at the trumpet's blast, he made the following proclamation: "The Roman Senate and Titus Quinctius their general, having conquered King Philip and the Macedonians, decree that the Greek states formerly subject to King Philip shall be free, exempt from tribute, and subject only to their own laws." The good news was too overwhelming to be grasped all at once. People could not believe their ears. They stared amazed at one another, as if they thought it was all a dream, and kept asking their neighbors for confirmation. The herald was recalled to repeat the proclamation, so eager were they to see, as well as hear, the announcer of their freedom. Then at last they believed the glad tidings, and the storm of applause and repeated cheers was clear proof that no blessing is dearer to the masses than liberty. For days afterward men marvelled that there was on earth a people who would at their own cost, their own toil and risk, go to war to win liberty for others—a distant overseas people at that—to abolish everywhere in the world injustice and tyranny, and bring to every land the mighty rule of justice, righteousness, and legality.

___

c. POLYBIUS: *Histories*, XXIX, 27

As King Antiochus was advancing against Ptolemy, . . . the Roman delegate Popillius came to meet him. Antiochus shouted a greeting from a distance and held out his hand in welcome, but Popillius held out the tablet containing the decree of the Senate and bade Antiochus read that first, not deigning to give him a friendly greeting before he knew whether the recipient chose to be friend or foe. But when the king, after reading the tablet, said he wanted to consult his friends about the situation, Popillius did something that was considered heavy-handed and arrogant to the last degree. He happened to have a vine stick in his hand; he drew a circle around Antiochus, and bade him reply to the despatch without stepping out of that ring. The king was taken aback by this haughty conduct, but after thinking it over for a moment replied that he would comply in full with the Romans' ultimatum. Then Popillius and his staff shook hands with him and treated him like a friend.

___

d. APOCRYPHA: *I Maccabees* VIII, 1-13
(Authorized Version)

Now Judas had heard of the fame of the Romans, that they were mighty and valiant men, and such as would . . . make a league of amity with all that came unto them. . . . It was told him also of their wars and noble acts which they had done among the Galatians, . . . and what they had done in the country of Spain for the winning of the mines of silver and gold which is there;

and that by their policy and patience they had conquered all the place, though it were very far from them; and the kings also that came against them from the uttermost part of the earth, till they had discomfited them, and given them a great overthrow, so that the rest did give them tribute every year; how also Antiochus the great king of Asia, . . . having an hundred and twenty elephants, with horsemen, and chariots, and a very great army, was discomfited by them. . . . It was told him besides, how they destroyed and brought under their dominion all other kingdoms and isles that at any time resisted them; but with their friends and such as relied upon them they kept amity; and that they had conquered kingdoms both far and nigh, insomuch as all that heard of their name were afraid of them.

———

e. CICERO: *Letters to his Brother*, I, 1, 8-25 (abridged)

It is splendid that you have governed Asia for three years without letting a single statue, picture, vase, garment, or slave tempt you from the straight and narrow path. Experience by now has taught you that you must answer also for the actions and even the words of your staff. They must not use for private gain the power you delegate to them to maintain their official position. As for you, let your ears have the reputation of hearing only what they hear, and not slanderous whispers motivated by hope of gain. Let your signet ring be not a mere instrument of another's will, but a guarantee of the firmness of your own. Let the whole province recognize that the welfare, families, reputation, and fortunes of all whom you govern are very precious to you, and that you will have nothing to do with either givers or takers of bribes. Let the cornerstones of your administration be, on your part, honesty and self-restraint, on the part of your staff, a sense of honor. Be circumspect but conscientious in your relations with provincials, and with Greeks, some of whom are dishonest and undependable, while others should be treated with the respect due to those from whom we Romans have learned so much. Keep your servants always firmly in hand. Be strict and impartial in administering justice; grant hearings readily, hand down decisions tactfully, hear and settle arguments scrupulously. My own opinion is that all who govern others must make their every act contribute to the maximum happiness of those they govern.

I see that everyone agrees you are being very conscientious: no new public debt; ruined cities rebuilt; no subversive activity; the cities governed by their aristocracies; highway robbery put down; the incidence of murder reduced; the reputation, fortunes, and peace of mind of the wealthy relieved from trumped-up prosecutions, that cruelest device of a governor's greed. I hear that your taxes are fair, that you grant audiences readily; in short, that your whole administration is a model of clemency, gentleness, and kindness of heart.

---

f. VERGIL: *Aeneid*, VI, 847-853
(Rolfe Humphries' translation, 1952)*

Others, no doubt, will better mould the bronze
To the semblance of soft breathing, draw from marble
The living countenance; and others plead
With greater eloquence, or learn to measure,
Better than we, the pathways of the heaven,
The risings of the stars; remember, Roman,
To rule the people under law, to establish
The way of peace, to battle down the haughty,
To spare the meek. Our fine arts, these, forever.

---

g. TACITUS: *Histories*, IV, 74

[*A Roman general speaks.*] "Wars between petty kings were always rife in Gaul before you yielded to us, to the rule of law. We, despite constant provocation, have used a victor's advantage only to levy upon you the cost of keeping the peace; for there can be no peace without armies, no armies without pay, and no pay without tribute. Everything else we share: you often command our

---

* Reprinted by permission from *The Aeneid: A Verse Translation* by Rolfe Humphries, Charles Scribners' Sons, New York, 1952.

legions, you govern this and other provinces; we are neither selfish nor exclusive. When our emperors are good, you profit as much as we, though you are far away; when they are wicked, their cruelty bears hardest on those close by. Endure your masters' extravagance and greed as you do unfruitful fields or heavy rains and other acts of God. There will be wickedness as long as there are men, but it does not last forever, and occasional better times are a compensation. . . . If the Romans are driven out, which God forbid, civil war is inevitable. Eight hundred years of luck and discipline have wrought this imperial fabric. It cannot be unraveled without destroying those who unravel it. And you will bear the brunt of it, for you have gold and prosperity, the chief causes of war. So love and cherish peace, and the City in which we both, victors and vanquished alike, have equal rights. Learn from history not to prefer revolt and ruin to docility and peace of mind."

---

h. TACITUS: *Agricola,* 30

[*A Scottish chieftain addresses his clansmen.*] "Whenever I ponder why we fight and where we stand, I have high hopes that your present unity will bring into being liberty for all Britain. Here you are, all free men; we are at the world's end; not even the sea is safe, for there looms against us the Roman fleet. Armed battle, once the brave man's glory, has become the coward's haven. Earlier battles against the Romans have been won and lost, but we, the last hope and mainstay, were always here, the pride of British stock, dwelling in her utmost fastnesses, no subject shores in view. . . . Now Britain's farthest marches are exposed, and the unknown is always impressive; but beyond us there is no clan; nothing but waves and rocks, and, deadlier still, Romans, whose arrogance no meekness, no moderation of yours can avoid. World-wide robbers, since the ransacked earth has nothing left to plunder, they cast greedy eyes on the sea. Rich enemies arouse their greed for gold; poor ones, their hankering for power. Neither East nor West has sated them; alone of men, they lust for the goods of rich and

poor alike. Robbery, murder, brigandage—they lie when
they call it Empire: they make a desert, and they call it
peace."

---

i. AELIUS ARISTIDES: *To Rome,* 59-60, 64-65, 101, 103, 104 (abridged)

Marvelous, unique in the world, is your magnificent
concept of citizenship. You have divided your whole
world Empire into two classes. Those of more culture,
pedigree, and influence you have everywhere made Roman citizens . . . ; the rest are your subjects. Distance
from Rome either by sea or by land makes no difference
to citizenship; Asia or Europe, it is all the same. No one
worthy of office or trust is an alien. A universal democracy has been established under one best ruler. . . .
No jealousy stalks your Empire. You yourselves have
set the example by sharing everything, and giving those
qualified the opportunity to rule when their turn comes,
as well as to be ruled. No hatred lurks among those left
out. Since the state is a commonwealth, and like a single
city, its governors naturally think of the governed not
as aliens, but as their own kith and kin. . . . You have
surveyed the whole world, built all sorts of bridges, cut
highways through mountains, filled the deserts with
hostels, and made everything civilized, systematic, and
orderly. . . . Before your rule everything was upside
down and drifting aimlessly, but under your charge con-
fusion and strife have ceased, everywhere order has
emerged, and the bright light of prosperity and good
government. Laws have been proclaimed, and the gods'
altars win men's confidence. . . . Now universal and
manifest freedom from fear has been granted to all the
earth and those that dwell therein. . . . The gods, beam-
ing upon your Empire, have had their part in its ordering
and confirm you in its possession.

THE ART OF WAR

To illustrate what made the Romans good soldiers. A veteran centurion summarizes his career [dramatic date 171 B.C.]; Plutarch pictures a Roman general's triumph [dramatic date, 167 B.C.]; Polybius describes the Roman army of the mid-second century B.C.; a Jewish historian, writing A.D. 75-79, comments on Roman military discipline; the Emperor Hadrian officially commends his troops after a review [A.D. 128]; and a late [fourth-fifth century A.D.] handbook describes recruit training.

✓　　　✓　　　✓

a. LIVY: *From the Founding of the City,* XLII, 34 (abridged)

"Fellow citizens, I, Spurius Ligustinus, am a Sabine. My father left me a half-acre of land and a small cottage. I was born and raised there, and I live there now. I have six sons and two married daughters. I first enlisted twenty-nine years ago. For two years I fought King Philip in Macedon as a private; the third year Flamininus promoted me to centurion for bravery. On discharge, I volunteered at once to go to Spain with Cato, a shrewd judge of valor, as old soldiers know. He appointed me first centurion of the first century. I volunteered for the third time for the army that beat King Antiochus, and again I was made first centurion. Then I served two hitches of a year each; after that, twice in Spain. After my first Spanish campaign, as a reward for valor, the general brought me home with him to march in his triumph; I served my second Spanish campaign because the general asked for me personally. I was chief centurion four times in a few years. I have had thirty-four

113

rewards from commanders for bravery. I have won six medals for saving fellow-soldiers' lives. I am over fifty and have served twenty-two years in the army. I have given you four soldiers [his grown sons] to replace me. But as long as any recruiting officer judges me fit for service, I will never ask for deferment."

---

b. PLUTARCH: *Life of Aemilius Paulus,* 32-34 (abridged)

Aemilius' triumph lasted three days. The first was hardly long enough for the display of captured statues, paintings, and colossal figures, mounted on 250 wagons. The second began with wagonloads of the finest Macedonian armor, bronze and iron, all highly polished and tastefully arranged so as to seem casually heaped. Then came 3000 men carrying silver money, in 750 containers weighing 180 pounds each, four men to a container. Others carried displays of heavy, embossed silverware. Early on the third day trumpeters blew the battle call. Young men followed them, in purple-bordered robes, leading to sacrifice 120 sleek, beribboned oxen with gilded horns. Boys carried libation vessels of silver and gold. Next came the gold-coin bearers, carrying seventy-seven 180 pound containers. Then came the bearers of the holy chalice made to Aemilius' order; it was gold, weighed 600 pounds, and was set with precious stones. Perseus' gold dinner-service, chariot, armor, and crown were also displayed. Then, after a short interval, his children passed, dressed as slaves, their retinue weeping, stretching out their hands to the spectators, and teaching the royal children, too, how to beg for mercy. Next came Perseus himself, dressed in black and seeming stunned and crazed by his great tragedy. Then were carried 400 gold crowns, sent by Greek cities with delegations to Aemilius in honor of his victory. Then Aemilius in person, standing in a splendidly decorated chariot, wearing gold and purple, and with a laurel branch in his right hand. His whole army, also carrying laurel branches, followed their general's chariot in formation, singing the traditional ribald songs, victory hymns, and praises of their commander.

c. POLYBIUS: *Histories*, VI, 19-39 (abridged)

An infantryman must serve for sixteen years before he is forty-six; in emergencies, for twenty. Those with an annual income of less than 400 drachmas [$80] are assigned to the navy. No one can hold political office unless he has finished ten years' military service. The consuls appoint annually a day on which all Romans of military age must present themselves. Their officers choose them by a rotation system which insures an even quality of men for each legion. A legion's strength is 4,200; in emergencies, 5,000. The recruits take an oath to obey their officers and do as they are told to the best of their ability. Simultaneously, the consuls proclaim to the Italian allied cities the number of men they require and the time and place at which the selectees must report.

They choose ten centurions according to merit, of whom the first is a member of the military council. They want centurions to be, not rash fire-eaters, but born leaders, steady, and of strong personality, who will stand firm in the pinches and die rather than surrender.

The Romans were quick to copy Greek weapons, for they have the unique virtue of readily changing outmoded practices and imitating what others do better.

On the appointed day, on which they have all sworn to report at the rendezvous, every recruit appears without fail; the only excuses are bad omens and physical unfitness. Then they pitch their camp, always and everywhere according to the same simple square plan, whose street layout and arrangement of buildings resemble a town.

Those convicted by courts-martial are cudgeled or stoned to death. Those who escape are pariahs. Cudgeling is the punishment also for theft, false witness, masturbation, and for those who have been punished three times for the same crime. Among cowardly acts unbecoming a soldier are reckoned lying about valor to gain distinction, deserting one's post, and cravenly throwing away one's weapons in battle. Consequently, troops often face certain death rather than leave their post, even when many times outnumbered, because they fear condign punishment.

The officers have invented an appropriate and terrible solution for wholesale cowardice. They line up the legion, order the cowards to step forward, give them a tongue-lashing, and, choosing about one in ten of the guilty, have them cudgeled unmercifully to death. Since all are equally subject to the fearful chance of drawing the fatal lot, this is the ideal deterrent and corrective.

Equally efficient are their incentives to raw recruits to run risks. The general assembles the troops, brings forward those who appear to have voluntarily acted above and beyond the call of duty, commends them, and rewards them. The first man over the wall of a besieged city gets a gold crown; so do those who have saved the lives of citizens or allies.

An infantryman's daily pay is two obols [ten cents], a centurion's twice that. An infantryman gets a monthly wheat ration of about two-thirds of a medimnus [a bushel]; the paymaster deducts from his pay a fixed sum for rations, uniform, and extra weapons.

----

d. JOSEPHUS: *The Jewish War*, III, 102-107

Their military experience fortifies the Romans in spirit as well as in body. Fear, too, is inculcated into the troops. Regulations lay down the death penalty for mere slovenliness as well as for desertion, and they fear their generals more than they do the regulations. High distinctions for bravery take the curse off cruelty for the offenders. Their perfect discipline is a model in peacetime; in battle, it unifies the whole army, so that their lines are compact, their wheeling maneuvers perfectly executed, their ears pricked to respond to orders, their eyes keen for signals, their hands ready for work. Superior numbers, stratagems, bad terrain, even bad luck, have never beaten them; for them, to win is a surer thing than to be lucky. They plan so well before they strike, the army follows the plan so effectively, that it is no wonder the boundaries of their Empire are the Euphrates on the east, the Ocean on the west, the richest part of Libya on the south, and the Danube and the Rhine on the north.

e. HADRIAN: Dessau, *Inscr. Lat. Sel.*, 2487, 9134 (abridged)

TO THE CAVALRY

Trenches which others take several days to dig, you finished in a day. You built a difficult wall, fit for permanent quarters, in not much longer that it takes to build one of turf. Turf. is cut to uniform size, is easy to carry and handle, and not hard to lay, being naturally soft and even. But you used big heavy stones of odd sizes, hard to carry, lift, and set. You have cut a straight moat through hard, coarse gravel, and leveled it off. . . .

TO THE FIRST PANNONIANS

You did everything smartly. You covered the area adequately in maneuvers. Your javelin throws were neatly executed, though short weapons are hard to handle. Several of you were equally good with the lance. You vaulted smartly into the saddle just now, and briskly yesterday. If there were anything amiss, it would not escape me; if there were anything outstandingly bad, I should notice. But I found your entire drill uniformly satisfactory. . . .

---

f. VEGETIUS: *Manual of Military Science,* I, 1,
3-6, 9, 10, 12, 19; II, 23 (abridged)

Greek superiority in techniques and intelligence is universally admitted. But we beat all comers by choosing recruits skillfully, teaching them the laws of war, hardening them by daily drill, anticipating actual battles in maneuvers, and punishing the lazy ones severely. Knowing military science contributes to combat readiness; no one is afraid to do what he feels he has learned well.

The best recruits are sturdy, unsophisticated country boys, just coming to manhood, and about five feet ten to six feet tall. But watch for bright eyes, good posture, broad chests, muscular shoulders, strong arms, longish fingers, flat stomachs, slim hips, sinewy legs; these are worth more than mere height.

Recruits should be taught to march, four miles an

hour in summer, five at quick step; to jump and to swim. The ancient Romans, who learned military science in the school of constant wars and dangers, chose the Field of Mars for drill. The Tiber was handy, for washing off the sweat and dust, and relaxing the recruits with a swim after a long march.

Teach recruits to thrust, not cut. A cut, however vicious, is not often fatal, but a thrust two inches deep is a mortal wound.

Recruits should be made to march in cadence, carrying weights up to sixty pounds, to prepare them for carrying rations as well as arms on hard campaigns.

It is not seniority that makes a soldier; no matter how many campaigns he has behind him, the undrilled man is still a recruit.

— Reading No. 5 —

CREATIVE BORROWING

A farcical scene between drunken slaves, out of a comedy by Plautus [200 B.C.], borrowed from the Greek, but with a strong Roman color; a long tragic lyric of Catullus, intricately wrought [about 55 B.C.]; Vergil's hymn on the birth of a child, also complex in structure, with a pattern of sevens [40 B.C.]; and an elegy of Propertius [about 23 B.C.], to illustrate the conventions and technique of Roman love poetry.

✓   ✓   ✓

a. PLAUTUS: *Stichus,* 641-772 (abridged)

Scene: Athens, a street with three houses.

Cast of Characters:

STICHUS	} slaves, just home with their masters
SANGARINUS	} from overseas
STEPHANIUM,	a maid

Enter STICHUS, *slightly drunk, and obviously on the lookout for someone. He arranges, unsteadily, a table and bench in front of one of the houses.*

STICH. (*Shading eyes with hand, and slurring his s's*). Silly business, seems to me, and stupid, this keeping an eye out for someone you're waiting for. Heaven's sake! That doesn't make them come a second faster. Yet here I am, keeping an eye peeled for Sangarinus, and it won't hurry him up one bit. By golly, I'll have this party by myself, if he doesn't show up. I'll just roll the wine barrel over here from our house, and then settle down to it. The day's melting away like snow.

119

Enter SANGARINUS, *airily.*

SANG. Hello, Athens, wet nurse of Greece, my master's home sweet home! Glad to see you! But I wonder about my girl, my pal-in-the-slave-quarters, Stephanium, how she is and what she's doing. I left it to Stichus to give her my best and tell her I'd be arriving today, so she'd have dinner ready on time. But speak of the devil. . . .

STICH. (*Rolling barrel, brandishing jug.*) Noble of my master, donating this donation to poor old Stichus. Gods above, what a barrel of pleasure I've got here, belly laughs, jokes, wet kisses, rock-and-roll, sweet nothings, and push-overs! (*He drinks.*)

SANG. How're you doing, Stichus?

STICH. Swell, Sangarinus, you old smoothie! We've got company, you and I (*patting the barrel*): the god of wine himself. Yep, by golly, dinner's ready, your master's house is liberty hall for you and me. There's a party at our house. (*Passes the jug.*) Here's a present someone gave me.

SANG. Who hit the jackpot?

STICH. Never mind; just hurry and get spruced up.

SANG. (*Hurt.*) I *am* spruced up!

STICH. Fine! This is our day to get well oiled. Down with foreign travel! Let's be hundred percent Athenians! (*He drinks.*) Follow me. (*Exit into house.*)

SANG. I'm with you. This is the way a homecoming ought to begin (*smacking his lips*). That first handout makes this my lucky day. (*Exit.*)

Enter STEPHANIUM *from the other house.*

STEPH. Ladies and gentlemen, for fear any of you should wonder why I'm coming out of this house when I live in that one, I'll tell you a secret. They sent for me a while ago to help out. I've had my hands full there setting the table and cleaning house, but I've not neglected my pals Stichus and Sangarinus; their dinner's ready. Stichus did the shopping, I'm doing the rest; it's his idea of division of labor. Now I'll go and take care of my homecoming boy friends. (*Exit into house: re-enter* SANG. *and* STICH.)

SANG. (*Pretending to be bossing a gang.*) Come on out: start the parade! Stichus, you're appointed Boss of the Barrel. I'm planning to attack this meal from all directions. It's mighty nice of them to let us have our party here. I want all passers-by invited.

STICH. O.K. Come one, come all—but with their own wine. For today's contributions from *this* (*patting the barrel*) go to us exclusively. Let's keep this a private party, just for you and me.

SANG. This is quite a spread for the money: nuts, tender young beans, baby figs, a bowl of olives, lupine, little canapés.

STICH. (*With drunken solemnity.*) It's plenty: a slave had better take it easy on expenses and not splurge. To each his own. (*Patting the barrel*). People who are in the chips drink out of rare goblets and snifters, we drink out of our little brown jug, but we do our duty by the drink all the same, as well as we can.

SANG. Come on, arrange the seating.

STICH. (*With mock politeness*). You take the head of the table. I'll split with you. Here, pick whatever department you like.

SANG. What's this with "department"?

STICH. What do you want to be head of, the Water Department or the Wine Department?

SANG. Wine—that's crystal clear! But while our girl, yours and mine, is slowing us down with her dolling up, let's have a little brawl of our own. You're elected commander-in-chief.

STICH. (*Slapping him on the back.*) I just thought of a good one: here we are, bench warmers instead of lounge lizards. We're like the Cynics; we always do it the hard way.

SANG. (*Lolling on his bench.*) No, no, don't mention it; life couldn't be softer. By the way, commander, what's holding up the jug? (*Reaches for it*). How many jiggers to a drink?

STICH. As many as the fingers on your hand. There's an old proverb, "Pour me five, pour me three, but never, no never, four jiggers for me."

SANG. (*Pours and drinks.*) Here's mud in your eye! (*Passes the jug.*) Pour yourself a half a jigger from the Water Department, if you know what's good for you. (*Pours another; sings.*)

Here's to thee and here's to me,

And here's to you (*He waves to the audience*) and here's
   to we,
And, to add to the total sum,
Here's to our little Stephanium.

STICH. (*Claps him on the back.*) Nice work! Here's
the jug; wet your whistle.

SANG. (*Wistfully.*) I could use a piece of steak.

STICH. (*Hurt.*) If what we've got's not good enough
for you, it's just tough. Have some water.

SANG. Sorry, you're right. I'm just a pig! (*Pours a jug-
ful for the stage musician.*) Here, Maestro, have a drink.
(*The musician refuses.*) By golly, you're going to drink
it; I won't take no for an answer. Take it, I tell you! It
won't cost you a penny; it's on the house. It's not like
you to be bashful. Take that flute out of your mouth!

STICH. When he's had his, you slow down to my
speed. I don't want this lapped up all at once. We'll be
good for nothing later on. (*Inspects barrel.*) Gad, you
can get through a barrel mighty fast!

SANG. (*As musician gives in.*) What do you say to that?
You took it hard, but it didn't kill you. Come on, Maestro,
you've had your drink, so flute to mouth, and blow out
your cheeks like a puff-adder. (*Musician plays;* SANGA-
RINUS *dances.*) Come on, Stichus, whoever fouls up the
step loses a round of drinks.

STICH. Fair enough. I'll always agree to an honest
proposition.

SANG. Come on, then, watch this. (*Whirls round and
round, then reels to bench.*) If you foul it up, I'll collect
on the spot.

STICH. Right as rain; couldn't be fairer. Here goes for
my first round. (*Dances and sings.*)

Enchantment it lends when rivals are friends.
Two to drink from a single glass.
Two to love the selfsame lass.
I'm you, you're me: we're as one as one can be.
Two guys, one doll; who she's with doesn't matter at all:
   Nobody's jealous of nobody.

(SANGARINUS *chimes in; they sing it* da capo.)

SANG. (*Tired out.*) Whoa! Whoa! Let's not run a good
thing into the ground. I want to play something else.

STICH. What do you say we call the girl friend out? She'll be glad to dance.

SANG. O.K. by me.

STICH. (*Bellowing.*) Stephanium! Sweetie! Dearie! Lovey-dovey! Come on out to your lover-boys! You've made yourself pretty enough for me.

SANG. You're the prettiest girl in the world.

STICH. We're feeling high; make us feel higher. Come on out and join the fun.

SANG. We're home from overseas, and we want you (*leering*), Stephanitsy-bitsy, my honey. If you want our love, if you want us both.

Enter STEPHANIUM, *patting her hair. They each take an arm and squire her to the table.*

STEPH. (*Ogling them.*) There's nothing I wouldn't do for you, my pets. So help me Venus, I'd have been out here with you long ago, but I wanted to look my best for you. Just like a woman: she bathes and scrubs and prinks and paints, and still feels a perfect flop. B.O. can ruin a party girl faster than personal daintiness can make her.

STICH. What a conversationalist!

SANG. The perfume of her words knocks me off my feet!

STICH. (*In torment.*) Sangarinus, I'm a total wreck!

SANG. (*Sympathetically.*) Total? Too bad!

STEPH. (*Provocatively.*) Which is my place?

SANG. Which place do you want?

STEPH. By both of you, for I love you both! (*Kisses each.*)

STICH. That remark has knocked my nest egg for a loop.

SANG. That remark will cost me my savings for freedom.

STICH. Oh, my aching back! So help me, Sangarinus, now she's just got to dance. Come my sweet honey-lamb, dance! I'll be your partner.

SANG. (*Reels toward them.*) You can't get away with that. I want to get a thrill too.

STEPH. Well, if I've got to dance, give the maestro a drink.

STICH. Yes, and ourselves too. (*Tilts the barrel.*)

SANG. There, Maestro, you first. Then, when it has hit the spot, get in the old groove, and slide into a smooth sexy song that'll make us tingle to our finger-tips. (*To* STICHUS.) Put in some water. (*To musician.*) Here you are, drink this. (*Musician obliges.*) Ah, his last shot went down well; this time he's not making such hard work of it. (*To* STEPHANIUM.) While he's drinking, apple of my eye, how about a nice wet kiss?

STICH. Hey! What do you think she is: a street-walker? To think of a fellow giving his girl a nice wet kiss, and both of them standing! (*Pushes them over onto the bench.*) Whoopee! Serves you right, you chiseler!

SANG. (*To musician.*) Come on, blow out your cheeks, and let's have something sweet and low-down. We gave you old wine; you give us new music. (*Musician outdoes himself; all dance wildly.*) Where's the ballet dancer or strip-tease artist that could match that?

STICH. (*Game to the last.*) Well, you beat me that time, but challenge me again!

SANG. (*Cutting more complicated capers.*) Just try this one!

STICH. And you try this one!

SANG. Hip, hip!

STICH. Pip-pip!

SANG. Flip-flip!

STICH. Whew!

SANG. Now both together! Bring on all your dirty competition! We love that music as a mushroom loves the rain.

STICH. (*Exhausted.*) Let's go in now! We've danced enough; our wine has given out. Ladies and gentlemen, clap hard and go have a brawl of your own! (*Exeunt omnes.*)

———

b. CATULLUS: *Poems*, 68b (tr. E. A. Havelock, 1939) *

* Reprinted from *The Lyric Genius of Catullus,* "The Flower Cut Down," by E. A. Havelock, Basil Blackwell, Publisher, Oxford, 1939.

I

No more refrain, O muse: declare the story
Of what I owe to Allius my friend.
Immortal may his honour stand, defying
The centuries' interminable trend.

Make of my voice a message heard of millions.
Wrinkled let this poor paper still proclaim
The unforgotten service that he rendered.
Let not time's dusty webs surround his name.

II

Thou knowest well how on my heavy spirit
Was laid a double anguish of desire,
How tasting sweets of love I tasted sorrow,
And mingled salt tears with volcanic fire.

Then it was he who ready came to save me,
Like a calm wind to bark by tempest blown.
He lent his house and home for assignation.
So were the barriers to love torn down.

III

At fall of eve my love came to the threshold.
She moved on whispering feet, a goddess fair.
Poised on the trodden stone she stayed her footfall,
    Watching me there.

Her shoe creaked—that was all—and I remembered
Laodamia to her love and lord
Arriving home and waiting in the doorway
    For his first word.

One hour of fellowship they had together,
Ere Trojan service summoned him from home.
So went the gallant flower of Grecian manhood,
Sailing to Troy and their untimely tomb.

IV

Still in that plain are bitter ashes buried.*
Alas for Troy! My brother's grave is there.
O brother, how uncomforted your passing:
How dark and comfortless my own despair!

You went, and all the fortunes of our household
Went with you and were buried with your clay,
And my own bliss, that lived by your affection,
    Died in a day.

And now far off in graveyard unfamiliar
Your lonely dust lies in an alien land.
The fateful soil of Troy holds you in keeping,
Laid by the margin of a foreign strand.

V

O dreamer Paris, lying with thy Helen
In stolen bowers of ease, dream thou no more.
The chivalry of Greece, for vengeance hasting,
With arms comes knocking at thy chamber door.

Laodamia, thou must leave thy lover.
Through thy life go with him, he must depart.
How fathomless the springs of thy affection!
How deep the tides that sweeping fill thy heart!

To bear the yoke of passionate submission
The heart of peerless woman still can learn.
Thy smouldering fires burn on, waiting to kindle
In that brief blissful hour of his return.

VI

Thine image lives again, as now before me
Here in this room another woman stands
Peerless and passionate and proud, yet yielding
    Into my hands.

Light of my life, see where the little Cupid
Clad in his yellow suit, with bow and dart,
Plays hide and seek about us as I clasp you
  Close to my heart.

VII

What though my love alone cannot content her?
She is discreet; her sins none other sees.
Why play the jealous fool? The queen of heaven
Herself must bear Jove's infidelities.

No flare of torches brought her to my dwelling;
No marriage-escort might her journey mark.
Stolen from husband's bed were her caresses,
The secrets murmured in the magic dark.

Of all her golden days can she remember
Some with a special quality of bliss?
Let her keep these for me. My short petition
  Asks only this.

VIII

Allius, sterling friend, my verse is ended
Which celebrates your service and your praise.
May fleet tomorrow's day and then tomorrow
Never your monument with rust erase.

The gods are just, and ever have rewarded
Men of true heart and faithful to their oath.
May you and she you love enjoy their blessing:
  Peace to you both.

Peace to that house of memories immortal
In springtime of our love that saw us meet,
Peace above all to that dear life that renders
  My own life sweet.

c. VERGIL: *Eclogue* IV

POLLIO

I

Muses, Sicily's band, let us make a loftier music!
Vineyards and low tamarisks do not always fit the occasion;
Let our shepherd song be resplendent enough for a consul.

II

The last age is at hand, prophesied by the Sibyl of Cumae:
Now, sublimely renewed, starts again the centuries' cycle,
Now maiden Justice revisits the earth, now again Saturn rules us.
Now high heaven vouchsafes us a child, the first-born of promise.
To this newly born child, in whose time the peoples of iron
Shall pass away from the earth, and a world-wide golden race flourish,
Chaste Diana, be kind: your Apollo comes into his kingdom.

III

Yours, Pollio, is the year of this glorious era's beginning;
Now will commence yet again the seasons' mighty progression.
With you to lead, every lingering trace of our sinning shall vanish;
The ceaseless weight of their fear shall oppress the nations no longer.
This child's birthright shall be the life of the gods; he shall see them
Intermingled with men half god, and himself be seen of them;
He shall inherit a pacified world through his father's uprightness.

IV

Child, your playthings the earth untilled shall lavish upon
  you:
Trailing tendrils of ivy, mixed with masses of foxglove,
Lily of Egypt, all intertwined with smiling acanthus.
Unforced, she-goats shall come to the fold for the milking,
Udders distended with milk; the herds shall not fear
  mighty lions.
Of itself, your cradle shall rain soft flowers upon you.
Serpents shall vanish from earth; poison-herbs that pre-
  tend to be harmless
Shall vanish; common as weeds shall spring up Assyrian
  balsam.
  When you can read of your father's feats, and the glory
    of heroes,
And are grown-up enough to know the meaning of genius,
Then, slow but sure, waving wheat shall ripen and turn
  pastures golden;
Without the touch of the sower, blushing grapes shall
  hang from the brambles,
And stubborn oaks shall exude as their sap the dew of the
  honey.
Still shall some slight taint of ancient iniquity linger,
To bid men tempt the sea in ships, put walls in a circle
Round about their towns, or gouge earth's face with deep
  furrows.
Then once again the helm will be manned; a new Argo
  will carry
Hand-picked heroes once more; there shall be recurrence
  of battles,
And once again in might to Troy shall be ordered Achil-
  les.
  Next, when strengthening time has at last matured you
    to manhood,
Gladly shall traders abandon the sea, and nautical pine-
  planks
Shall not ply with their freight: each land with each crop
  will be teeming.
The earth shall not suffer the hoe, nor the vine the hook
  of the pruner;

The sturdy ploughman, too, shall lift the yoke from his
oxen.

Wool shall not learn masquerades, as now, in counterfeit
colors,

But the ram, of himself, in the meadow shall blush of a
sudden

Bright red, or all at once his fleece will turn saffron yellow.

Lambs as they feed shall discover themselves in a suit of
vermilion.

V

"Run on, run on, ages like these," said the Fates to their
spindles,

Voicing as one the will of the gods predestined and stead-
fast.

Enter upon your lofty career, for the time is approaching,

Dearest child of the gods, whose seed shall be godlike
children.

Look now; see how the mass of the vaulted firmament
trembles,

Land and reaches of sea and all the depth of the heavens;

Look how all things rejoice at the happy age that is coming!

VI

O that to me the last days of a long, long life may be
granted,

And breath not too scant to sing the praise of your prow-
ess:

Orpheus of Thrace should never then outdo me in singing,

Nor should Linus, though they get the help of mother
and father:

Orpheus of Calliope, and Linus of handsome Apollo.

Even Pan, if he vies with me, and Arcady judges,

Should, with Arcady judging, confess himself to be
beaten.

VII

Learn, baby boy, to greet with a smile the approach of
your mother,

Who for ten weary months has borne her pregnancy's
    burden.
Learn, baby boy! A child that does not smile on his
    parents,
No god honors with feasts, nor any goddess with love-
    play.

———

d. PROPERTIUS: *Elegies,* III, xvi (tr. Ezra Pound, 1917)[*]

Midnight, and a letter comes to me from our mis-
    tress:
Telling me to come to Tibur: At once!!
"Bright tips reach up from twin towers,
Anienan spring water falls into flat-spread pools."
What is to be done about it?
    Shall I trust myself to entangled shadows,
Where bold hands may do violence to my person?

Yet if I postpone my obedience
                because of this respectable terror,
I shall be prey to lamentations worse than a noc-
    turnal assailant.
And I shall be in the wrong,
                and it will last a twelve month,
For her hands have no kindness me-ward;

Nor is there anyone to whom lovers are not sacred
    at midnight
    And in the Via Sciro.
If any man would be a lover
                he may walk on the Scythian coast,
No barbarism would go to the extent of doing
    him harm,
The moon will carry his candle,
                the stars will point out the stumbles,
Cupid will carry lighted torches before him
                and keep mad dogs off his ankles.

* Reprinted by permission from *Personae* by Ezra Pound,
    New Directions, Norfolk, Conn., and Faber & Faber,
    Ltd., London.

Thus all roads are perfectly safe
                          and at any hour;
Who so indecorous as to shed the pure gore of a
    suitor?
    Cypris is his cicerone
What if undertakers follow my track,
                          such a death is worth dying.
She would bring frankincense and wreaths to my
    tomb,
    She would sit like an ornament on my pyre.

God's aid, let not my bones lie in a public location
With crowds too assiduous in their crossing of it;
For thus are tombs of lovers most desecrated.

May a woody and sequestered place cover me with
    its foliage
Or may I inter beneath the hummock
                          of some as yet uncatalogued sand;
At any rate I shall not have my epitaph in a high
    road.

— Reading No. 6 —

THE ROMAN CHARACTER

Some strong personalities, male and female, exemplifying some of the traits of character which have to be taken into account in assessing the Roman mind: self-sacrifice for the state [Decius, 340 B.C.]; fidelity to one's word, even unto death [Regulus, 250 B.C.]; austerity [Cato the Elder, 184 B.C.]; affability and reserve [Julius Caesar and Cato the Younger, 63 B.C.]; heroism and loyalty in a wife [43 B.C.]; modesty and righteous indignation in an emperor [Claudius, A.D. 41]; and dedication to scholarship [Pliny the Elder, died A.D. 79].

✓   ✓   ✓

a. LIVY: *From the Founding of the City,* VIII, 9

As the Roman lines were wavering, Decius, the Consul, shouted in a carrying voice, "We need the gods' help, Marcus Valerius. Come, then, state pontiff of the Roman people, let me say after you the formula of self-sacrifice to save the legions." Following the pontiff's instructions, he put on the purple-bordered toga, veiled his head, thrust one hand out from under the toga to touch his chin, stood on a spear, and said, "Janus, Jupiter, Father Mars, Quirinus, Bellona, Lares, divinities both native and foreign, ye gods whose power is over us and our enemies, and ye, divine shades of our ancestors, I, humbly beseeching your favor, pray that you may grant victory to the Roman people's arms, and visit their enemies with fear, trembling, and death. Asking this in the name of our Republic, army, legions, and allies, I consign the enemy's legions and allies, together with myself, to the divine shades and to death." After this prayer he bade his lictors go announce at once to his colleague Titus Manlius his self-sacrifice to save the army. Then he girt up his toga, put a fold of it over his head, vaulted in armor onto his horse, and plunged into the thick of the enemy.

———

b. HORACE: *Odes* III, 5, 13-56

Regulus, a captured Roman general sent home by the Carthaginians to propose to the Senate an exchange of prisoners, advised against it. Then, having given his word to return, he went back to Carthage to face the music.

His land's dishonor Regulus' mind foresaw.
Against the foe's vile offer he spoke his mind:
    Accepting it would mean for Romans
        Ruin and shame in succeeding ages.

Death, death must be the fate of our captured youth
But ransom never. "Flaunted on temple walls,
    I saw our flags, our arms surrendered;
        Craven," he said, "were the troops that lost them.

"Yes, I have seen our citizens trussed, their arms
Fast bound behind their backs; and Punic gates
    Left wide ajar in scorn, and farms now
        Tilled without fear, though our troops had burned
        them.

"Think not that men you ransom for gold will come
Home crying, 'Vengeance!' Squandering gold won't save
    Our face. As wool, once dyed, can never
        Gain back its natural, honest color,

"So, once the sense of honor has left the ranks,
It comes no more to dwell in unworthy breasts.
    If, loosed from snares, shy stags show spirit,
        Then there'll be fight in the men you ransom,

"Who put their faith in enemy faithlessness.
You cannot use to fight on another day
    The men whose wrists have felt the handcuffs,
        Cowardly oafs who object to dying.

"Poltroons, all such. They value their lives too high;
They don't know war is serious. Shame, O shame,
   That we should make a perch for Carthage
     Pinnacled high on our own dishonor!"

He turned, men say, from wife's and from children's kiss;
As though he felt he did not deserve them now,
   Unclasped their arms. With eyes cast downward,
     Stiff upper lip, and a hero's courage,

In Senate halls he buttressed some weak backbones—
Advice like his had never before been giv'n—,
   Then, through the ranks of grieving comrades,
     Elbowed his way into noble exile.

Well knowing what the barbarous torturer
Had waiting for him, yet did he thrust aside
   His kin who begged him not to go, and
     Crowds of the plebs who had blocked his passage,

As though, some weary case of a client o'er,
He'd planned a well-earned holiday for himself:
   A southern tour to visit farmlands,
     Or, for a sightseeing trip, Tarentum.

———

c. LIVY: *From the Founding of the City,* XXXIX, 40

The plebeian Marcus Porcius Cato far outshone all
other candidates for the censorship, patrician or plebeian,
no matter how distinguished their families. He had such
force of character and intelligence that, whatever his
station in life, his own efforts would have made him
famous. He lacked no talent of civic or private life: he
was as shrewd in the market place as he was as a farmer.
Legal knowledge, oratorical skill, or military success are
the usual roads to preferment: his was a genius so versa-
tile and all-embracing that whatever he turned his hand
to, he seemed to have been born to it. As a soldier, he
was the soul of courage, decorated for many distinguished
battles; when he was promoted to command, he was without peer as a general. In peacetime, if legal advice was

needed, he was an expert; if there was a case to be
argued, he was a master of eloquence, and his eloquence
did not die with him; . . . it still lives and flourishes,
immortalized in his various works. Speeches of his survive
in self-defence, in defence of others, and for the prosecution, for his opponents found his arguments as devastating
as his indictments. He was much attacked, and did much
attacking; whether the nobles bore down on him more
than he irritated the nobility would be hard to say.
Granted, he was irritable, too free-spoken and sharp-
tongued. But he was completely incorruptible, of in-
flexible integrity, and he despised both wealth and power.
In frugality, in endurance of toil and danger, he was a
man of iron spirit; not even old age, that universal slack-
ener, could break it. At eighty-six he wrote and delivered
his own defence, at ninety he indicted Servius Galba before the People's Court.

---

d. SALLUST: *Catiline,* 53-54

Thinking it over, I concluded that the distinguished
excellence of a minority among us has . . . brought
about the triumph of poverty over wealth, of few over
many. Even after soft living and laziness produced civic
decline, our country was still great enough to survive the
vices of its civil and military leaders, yet, like a mother
too old for childbirth, Rome for many years produced
almost no one of real excellence. But I can remember
two men of infinite excellence but different personality,
Cato and Caesar, . . . whose nature and character I shall
expound with all the skill at my command.

They were about equally matched in pedigree, years,
eloquence, loftiness of mind, and reputation, but their
reputations differed. Caesar's claim to greatness was his
good works and openhandedness; Cato's the consistency
of his conduct. Caesar grew famous for sympathic kindliness; Cato's reserve enhanced his prestige. Caesar won
fame for gifts, relief, and pardons; Cato, for never
wasting his money. The one was a refuge for the down-
and-out, the other the terror of the wicked. Men praised
the affability of the one, the steadiness of the other.
Finally, Caesar always worked hard and kept long hours;

in his concentration on his friends' interests he neglected his own; he never denied anyone any gift worth giving. What he wanted most was a high command, an army, a new war where his talents might shine. But Cato aimed at moderation, decorum, and above all at aloofness, never competing in riches with the rich, nor in party politics with the politician, but with the industrious in excellence, with the temperate in morality, with the guiltless in unselfishness; he preferred to *be* good rather than to seem so, and so the less he courted reputation, the more it followed in his train.

---

e. ANONYMOUS: *Funeral Eulogy* (Dessau, *I.L.S.*, 8393, abridged)

Rare are marriages so enduring, broken only by death, not divorce. Ours lasted forty-one years without a quarrel. I wish that I as the elder had died first. No need to record your wifely virtues: you were continent, dutiful, a true companion; you spun your wool, were devout without fanaticism, well groomed without ostentation, loving and affectionate to kinsfolk and household alike, as devoted to my mother as to your own parents. You had innumerable other virtues in common with every Roman married woman who values her reputation; you also had virtues that were unique. You provided funds for my escape by selling your jewels, stripping yourself of your gold and pearls. You duped our adversaries' spies and saw to it that I lacked for nothing in my exile. You made private plans, held secret meetings. A surprise message from you awoke me to the immediate threat of danger; your advice saved my life. You provided a safe hiding-place for me. When Marcus Lepidus objected to my pardon, you threw yourself at his feet. He treated you like a common slave; your body was covered with bruises. Yet with unflinching courage you braved brutal insult and injury and denounced him publicly. He was branded as responsible for my troubles, and soon paid the price for his deeds. Your courage had its effect: it brought an amnesty from Caesar. When peace came to the world again and the Republic was restored, ours was a quiet and happy life. . . .

f. CLAUDIUS: *Letter to the Alexandrians*
(Pap. Mus. Brit. 1912, abridged)

I pray you not to appoint a high priest to me and build me temples: I do not wish to be burdensome to my fellow men, and I hold that temples and things of that sort have always been reserved as special homage to the gods alone. . . . As for your quarrel, or breach of the peace, or, if I must be blunt, war, with the Jews, while reluctant to look into the responsibility for it too deeply, I have stored up within me an implacable anger against any who start further trouble. I tell you frankly that if you do not stop this suicidal and bigoted squabbling with each other, I shall be forced to demonstrate what a humane prince can be like when he turns to righteous indignation. . . .

----

g. PLINY THE YOUNGER: *Letters,* III, v, 8-17 (abridged)

My uncle would begin studying by lamplight before dawn in summer; in winter between midnight and two o'clock. He had trained himself to break his working hours with cat-naps. After a simple, old-fashioned breakfast, he would take a sun bath in summer, if time permitted, and have a book read aloud, while he took notes. He always copied out passages, maintaining that no book was so bad as not to have something of value in it somewhere. Then he would have a cold bath, a light lunch, and a very short siesta, after which, as though it were another day, he would work again until dinnertime. During dinner he would listen to reading and dictate notes rapidly. I remember once the reader mispronounced something, and a dinner guest made him go back and repeat it. "You understood him, didn't you?" said my uncle. The guest nodded. "Then why did you make him repeat? Your interruption has cost us ten lines." Such was his economy of time. It was his fixed and almost statutory habit, in summer, to get up from dinner before sunset, in winter, within an hour after. All this despite his official duties and the noise of city traffic. In the country, he would exempt from study only his actual bath time; even while undressing or being dried he would listen to something read, or dictate. On trips, with other things off his mind, he would concentrate on his studies, at his side a secretary with book and note pad. In winter, he wore gloves, so that not even biting cold could steal work time. In Rome he used a sedan chair. I recall his criticizing me for walking: "You might have avoided wasting those hours." He thought all time not spent on study was wasted. By such concentration he turned out 102 volumes, and left me 160 notebooks of extracts, written on both sides in a minute hand.

THE SEAMY SIDE

Passages to illustrate graft and political corruption. A war-contract fraud [dramatic date 212 B.C.]; an extract from a law against extortion [122 B.C.]; a vignette of the most corrupt of Roman governors [73 B.C.]; passages from his brother Quintus' letter of advice to Marcus Cicero on how to canvass for the consulship [64 B.C.]; a picture of corruption in Rome in the following year; a fragment of private accounts itemizing payment of protection money to the police [about A.D. 150-200]; a municipal ordinance against the black market in money [about A.D. 210]; and an angry outburst against extortion, from the Theodosian Code [A.D. 331].

✦   ✦   ✦

a. LIVY: *From the Founding of the City*, XXV, 3, 9-14; 4, 8-10 (abridged)

Postumius was a tax-collector who for many years had [almost] no equal in Rome for greed and the practice of graft. . . . The government having undertaken to insure against loss from storms any cargoes consigned to the armies, [he and his partner] would report shipwrecks that never happened. Those that did happen were no accidents, but deliberately engineered by the partners in the interests of graft. They would load old, battered hulks with a small, valueless cargo and sink them on the high seas, having first taken off the crews in lifeboats standing by for the purpose. Then they would present a padded bill for damages many times the cargo's actual value. Though this sharp practice had been indicted the year before to the praetor . . . , and reported by him to the Senate, no

action was taken, the Senators being reluctant to an-
tagonize the tax-collectors in wartime. The people proved
more ruthless against graft: two plebeian tribunes, . . .
finally spurred to take official notice of the nasty scandal,
proposed for Postumius a fine of 2,000 *asses*. Postumius
jumped bail, was declared an exile, interdicted from fire
and water, and his property confiscated.

b. Law on Extortion: *Corpus of Latin Inscriptions, I²,*
583, lines 1-4

If any person having served as dictator, consul, praetor,
master of the horse, censor, aedile, plebeian tribune,
quaestor, commissioner for capital cases, public land-
grant commissioner, military tribune of Legions I-IV, or
any son of the aforesaid, or any person who, or whose
father, is a senator, has, in the exercise of public office
or duly constituted authority, carried off, seized, exacted,
embezzled, or misappropriated a sum of money exceeding
. . . sesterces in any one year from any person who is
an ally, either with Latin rights or as a foreigner, under
the sovereignty, rule, authority or friendship of the Roman people, from the said person or from his king, people, or parent, or from persons now or hereafter obligated
to him or to his parent in authority, possession, or legal
ownership, or from any person to whom he or his parent
or son stands as heir, such person shall have the right to
sue or summon. The praetor shall conduct an investigation, and the trial, verdict, and assessment of damages
shall be the duty of such persons as under this law shall
constitute the court.

c. M. CICERO: *Against Verres,* II, v, 27; 86

When spring began, . . . Verres would devote himself
to arduous circuit-riding, so sturdily and briskly that no one
ever saw him on horseback. He rode like the old kings
of Bithynia, carried by eight bearers in a sedan chair
cushioned with translucent brocade stuffed with rose
petals. He wore one garland for his head, another round
his neck, and he would keep smelling at a fine dotted
linen gauze bag full of rose petals. Whenever, at the end

of a day's stage, he came to a town, he would be carried
in the same sedan chair straight to his bedroom, . . .
whither suits at law were brought to him secretly, and
whence decisions were shortly afterward brought away
openly. Then when he had done his praetor's duty briefly
in his bedroom, to the credit more of his bank account
than of his reputation for equity, he spent the rest of his
time discharging his duty to Venus and Bacchus. . . .
In his capacity as admiral, this Roman governor would
waver drunkenly on the beach in slippers, wearing a
purple Greek cloak and an ankle-length tunic, and leaning
on one of his women.

----

d. Q. CICERO: *Brief Notes on Electioneering,* 41, 50, 52, 54

To gain popular favor the candidate must know the
voters by name, flatter and pay court to them, be generous, spread publicity, and awaken their hopes of government employment. . . .

Generosity is a broad topic. Perhaps your private income cannot reach the whole electorate, but your friends
benefit, and the mob is pleased. Give banquets and have
your friends give them, both to a random guest list and
to the electorate tribe by tribe. . . .

As for publicity, spread the word widely that you speak
well, that the tax-collector and the middle class like you,
the nobles wish you well, the young men crowd about
you, likewise clients you have defended, and the host
of men from the country towns who have come to Rome
expressly for your campaign. Let the voters say and
think that you know them well, call them affably by
name, unceasingly and conscientiously seek their vote,
are generous and open-handed, that even before dawn
your house is full of well-wishers, that all classes are in
your retinue, that you have made promises to everybody
and actually fulfilled them to many. . . .

Let your campaign, if at all possible, raise against your
competitors damaging suspicions, appropriate to their
personalities, of crime, vice, or bribery. , . .

Remember that this is Rome, a city made up of a con-
course of nations, full of frame-ups, chicanery, and vice
of every kind, where you must endure on every hand ar-

rogance, insult, ill-will, disdain, hatred, and importunity. It takes, I think, much common sense and dexterity for one and the same man to evade antagonisms, gossip, and frame-ups, and adapt himself to such a variety of personalities, viewpoints, and interests.

---

e. SALLUST: *Catiline,* 37

The common people generally, as one would expect from their character, supported Catiline's schemes. For invariably in politics the poor resent good men and support the wicked, hate the old order, long for the new, and, loathing their own lot, are eager to change everybody else's. Amid riot and treason they have no worries about supporting themselves, since poverty is a position not hard to keep up without a deficit.

Many things contributed to making the city plebs hotheaded. Rome was like a sewer into which had flowed from all over Italy brazen slanderers, unseemly wastrels, criminals and reprobates who found home too hot to hold them. Many, recalling how Sulla's victory had made some common soldiers senators, others rich enough to live in banqueting and luxury like kings, hoped for a similar reward of victory if they took up arms now. Young men who had formerly made ends meet as farm laborers were now attracted by private and public doles, and preferred idleness in town to hard work in the country. These and all the others waxed fat on their country's ills.

---

f. ANONYMOUS: Egyptian Village Accounts. *Revue de Philologie,* 3rd series, XVII (1943) 111

To military policeman		2 drachmas 1 obol
Bribe	240	"
Suckling pig	24	"
To policeman	20	"
For shakedown	2200	"
To informers (2)	100	"
To Hermias, informer	100	"
To	2574	" 3 obols

Second six months

To soldier on demand	500	drachmas
Premium for changing money	12	"
8 flagons wine @ 10 drachmas		
⅛ obol	. . . .	
To chief of police	. . . .	
Irrigation tax	1	drachma
Pasturage tax	1	"
To soldier on demand	400	drachmas
Premium for changing money	15	"

---

g. Ordinance from Mylasa, Asia Minor, Regulating Black Market: F. F. Abbott and A. C. Johnson: *Municipal Administration in the Roman Empire* (Princeton, 1926) p. 461, No. 133, lines 15-36

If anyone, free or slave, in any way whatsoever, except the renter and manager of the bank, is caught exchanging or buying money, he shall be brought before the banker upon indictment before the council by any citizen. When convicted before the magistrates and council, if the transaction involved no premium, the banker and the informer-prosecutor shall be entitled to the money; the banker shall also be entitled to exact payment as previously guaranteed. If the transaction involved a premium, a freeman shall pay to the most sacred fisc of our most divine masters the emperors a fine of 500 *denarii,* to the city treasury 250 *denarii,* to the informer-prosecutor 100 *denarii,* and the sum ascertained to be involved shall be forfeit to the bank. If a slave is convicted as aforesaid, he shall be yielded up by his master to the magistrates at a council meeting, shall receive fifty lashes, be thrown into prison, and confined for six months. Any master not complying shall himself be liable for the fines aforesaid to the most sacred fisc, the city treasury, and the informer-prosecutor.

---

h. *Theodosian Code,* I, 16, 7

The greedy hands of government employees shall stop immediately; I repeat, they shall stop. If after this warning they do not stop, they shall be lopped off with the sword. Admission fees to the judge's chambers shall not be charged, nor scandalous secret bribes for priority of hearings. Seeing the governor shall involve no fee. The judges' ears shall be open equally to paupers and the rich. The "chief clerk" shall not charge a fee for letting petitioners in; minor clerks shall not extort tips from litigants. The unbearable aggressiveness of centurions and other officials demanding small and large bribes shall be trampled down. The inexhaustible greediness of those delivering copies of records to litigants shall be moderated. The governor shall keep watch night and day against exactions from litigants by the aforesaid employees. Whosoever dares to ask for bribes in civil cases shall be punished by immediate force of arms, which shall sever the rascal's head from his neck. All victims of extortion shall have opportunity to testify before the governor. Against equivocators we authorize all persons to complain to our Imperial officers in the provinces, or to the Praetorian Prefects, if they are handier, so that, informed by their reports, we may take appropriate action against such gangsterism.

CONSERVATISM REVISITED

Selections illustrating Roman conservatism in theory and practice. First, chronology is violated to let a Roman of 221 B.C. list the ten conservative ideals. Then an aristocratic Roman clan takes on a war single-handed [dramatic date 479 B.C.]; a Greek historian sees aristocracy predominant in the Roman Republic [about 150 B.C.]; Cicero defines conservatism [56 B.C.], describes the benefits of aristocratic government, shows why a New Conservatism of intellectuals deserves to rule, and shows how a conservative government can with impunity permit the secret ballot [all 52-51 B.C.]. Finally, the same author distinguishes aristocratically, not to say snobbishly, between vulgar and gentlemanly pursuits [44 B.C.].

✓   ✓   ✓

a. PLINY THE ELDER: *Natural History,* VII, 139-140

Quintus Metellus, in the written version of his funeral eulogy over his father, the pontiff Lucius Metellus, who had been consul twice, dictator, master of the horse, and land-grant commissioner, and who was the first to include elephants in a triumphal procession (after the First Punic War), recorded that his father had realized the ten highest ideals which intelligent men spend their lives pursuing: to be a first-class warrior, an excellent speaker, a valiant general; to direct important policy, to win the highest office, to show supreme intelligence, to be judged the best senator, to make a large fortune honorably, to leave many children, and to be widely celebrated as a statesman.

b. LIVY: *From the Founding of the City,* II, 48-49

Then the Fabian clan went before the Senate. The consul, their spokesman, said, "Senators, as you know, the war with Veii needs constant attention rather than a large force. Worry about your other wars, and let the Fabii attend to Veii. We guarantee that the majesty of the Roman name will be safe there. We intend to wage this war at our own expense, like a family feud, let the state be free to employ its funds and forces elsewhere." After a hearty vote of thanks, the consul, emerging from the senate house, was escorted home by a file of Fabii who had waited in the senate antechamber for the result of the voting. After receiving orders to report under arms next day at the consul's door, they dispersed to their homes.

The news spread all over town; the Fabii were praised to the skies, because a single family had undertaken a community burden, and turned the war with Veii into a private responsibility discharged with private arms. If the city had two more clans with the same hearts of oak, one might tackle the Volsci single-handed, the other the Aequi, and the Roman people might enjoy peace and quiet while all their neighbors were being subjected.

Next day the Fabii took up arms and reported to their rendezvous. The consul, coming out in his red cloak, saw his whole clan drawn up in battle array before his door; they gathered round him and he gave the marching order. An army smaller in number or mightier in fame and popular admiration had never marched through Rome: 306 soldiers, all patricians, all of one clan, any one of whom you would have welcomed as a leader, and who as a group would have made a pre-eminent Senate in any period, were going out threatening doom to Veii with the thews and sinews of a single family.

---

c. POLYBIUS: *Histories,* VI, 11, 13

If we should focus on the power of the consuls, the constitution would seem completely monarchical; . . . if on that of the Senate, aristocratic rather; if on that of the people, it would seem to be clearly democratic. . . .

The Senate, first of all, controls the treasury, regulating its income and expenditures. The quaestors cannot make a single disbursement, except to the consuls, without a Senate decree. Even the heaviest . . . expense of all, the censors' quinquennial budget for constructing or repairing public works, is controlled by the Senate, which allots the necessary sum to the censors. Also, jurisdiction over crimes committed in Italy and needing public investigation; e.g., treason, subversive activity, poisoning, and murder, belongs to the Senate. Besides, if any private citizen or city in Italy needs arbitration, indemnity, assistance, or protection, all this is the Senate's responsibility. If a delegation is needed to a country outside Italy, to make an armistice, offer advice, issue injunctions, receive submission, or declare war, the Senate provides for it. Likewise, when delegations come to Rome, the Senate handles all questions of how to treat each one and what response to give it. With all of the foregoing the people have nothing whatever to do, so that when one is in Rome during the consul's absence, the constitution seems to be completely aristocratic. Many Greek states and many kings believe this, since the Senate has authority over practically all dealings with them.

---

d. CICERO: *For Sestius,* 96-98

Two classes of people have always existed in Rome, anxious to participate in politics and achieve distinction: one has wanted to be, and to be considered, representatives of the common people [*populares*]; the other, of the best people [*optimates*]. Those who wanted, in deed and word, to please the rank and file were regarded as *populares;* those whose conduct sought the approval of every good citizen were considered *optimates.* Well, who are these "best people"? Too many to count, and indispensable: initiators of public policy [*principes*], and their supporters; members of the upper classes, eligible for the Senate; citizens of the small towns and country districts; businessmen; even freedmen are *optimates.* Widespread and heterogeneous as its members are, this class as a whole . . . can be briefly . . . defined. All men are *optimates* who stand for law and order, are not naturally depraved, fanatical, or involved in domestic difficulties. Those whom you [of the opposition] called a "clique" are in fact honest, solid, family men. Those who in governing the state consult the wishes, interests, and opinions of this group are counted as defenders of the *optimates* and are *optimates* themselves, solid, superior citizens and initiators of public policy. What then is the landmark on which these helmsmen of the ship of state should fix their eyes, and by which they should plot their course? The most valuable and desirable one for all right-thinking, loyal, well-to-do citizens: peace with honor. Those who want this are all *optimates;* those who make it a reality are statesmen, preservers of the commonwealth. But men should not let their ambition for honor prompt them to disturb the peace, nor let their desire for peace and quiet dampen their ambition for honor. The corner-stones and bases of peace with honor, which initiators of public policy must protect and defend even with life itself, are these: religious observances, omens, magistrates' powers, senatorial prestige, laws, traditions, due process, financial credit, provinces, allies, glory of empire, armed forces, treasury.

----

e. CICERO: *On the Republic,* I, 53-54

What can be more glorious than virtue governing a state? Then the ruler of others is not himself the slave of any passion, but has developed within himself every virtue which he has prescribed and recommended for his fellow-citizens. Such a man imposes on his people no laws which he does not obey himself; he sets up his own life as their norm. If one person could achieve all these ideals, a plurality of rulers would be unnecessary; if the masses could see and agree upon the ideal, an élite of initiators of public policy [*principes*] would not be required. The causes of power-shifts from a king to a larger number, and from the many to the few, are respectively the difficulty of initiating policy and the erratic instability of popular assemblies. Thus aristocracies [*optimates*] have come to occupy a completely middle-of-the-road position between monarchy's weakness and democracy's instability. Aristocratic governors guarantee the greatest happiness of their citizens, who take their ease and leave all worrisome brain-work to other, responsible persons, who must never let the people think that the *principes* are neglecting the public interest. Equality of opportunity, that watchword of free peoples, is impossible to maintain; even democracies, however radical, are notorious for wide division of powers, which involves rigid selection of men for offices. . . . When the highest and the lowest (and every nation must contain both categories), get equal honor, equity itself is most inequitable, but in aristocracies this cannot happen.

---

f. CICERO: *On the Laws,* I, 22-23

That provident, sagacious, complex, sharp-witted animal, so retentive, reasonable, and intelligent, whom we call man, has been brought to birth by God the all-highest in very exalted circumstances. For he alone of all living species shares in the power of reason and intelligence, which the others entirely lack. Now what is more divine than reason in all heaven and earth? (I shall not rest my case on man alone.) Mature and perfected reason is properly called intelligence. Since this superlative intelligence exists in both man and God, the prime link between man and God is intelligence. Those who share intelligence share directive intelligence also. Law, then, being directive intelligence, . . . links men with the gods. Those who share law share justice also, and . . . belong to the same state, especially if they obey the commands of the same authorities. They obey this heavenly hierarchy, this divine mind, this omnipotent God, so that this whole universe ought to be considered a single state shared by gods and men. And, as in states . . . family relationships determine one's status, so in nature, but much more magnificently and pre-eminently, men are bound together by their [intellectual] relationship to the gods.

---

g. CICERO: *On the Laws,* III, 38-39

My granting the people the freedom to vote is so managed that the possession and use of political power shall be in the hands of the aristocracy. My law on voting ran as follows: "The vote shall be known to the aristocracy, and open to the plebeians." Its intention is to cancel all recent legislation which may in any way protect the secrecy of the ballot by forbidding the inspection, questioning, or challenging thereof, as for example Marius' law made the approaches to the polling places narrow. If these laws are made, as is usually the case, to prevent dishonest elections, I have no fault to find, but if it is true that they are not strong enough to stop electoral corruption, then by all means let the people have the ballot as a guarantee of their liberty, as long as it is offered voluntarily for inspection to any really substantial aristocratic citizen, so that liberty may consist in the very fact that the people are given an opportunity of honorably gaining the favor of the aristocracy.

---

h. CICERO: *On Duty,* I, 150-151 (abridged)

The standard distinction between vulgar and gentlemanly occupations is this. Tax-collecting or money-lending, which incur the hatred of mankind, are especially disapproved. Vulgar and unbecoming a free man is all unskilled labor for wages, where the wages carry with them the obligation of servitude. Those who buy from wholesalers for immediate resale are vulgar: their profit depends on misrepresentation, which is low and mean. All craftsmen are involved in vulgar skills, for there is nothing gentlemanly about a workshop. Trades that minister to pleasure—fishmongers, butchers, chefs, sausage-stuffers, fishermen, perfumers, dancers, gamblers—are definitely disapproved. But skills involving greater intelligence or utility, like medicine, architecture, or teaching liberal arts, are honorable for those to whose social class they are appropriate. Commerce on a small scale is vulgar, but if it is heavily capitalized, operates over a wide area, and benefits many people without misrepresentation, it is not much subject to criticism. If a merchant has a country estate to go to, it may even seem possible to justify praising him. Of all profitable occupations, there is none better, richer, pleasanter, worthier of man and gentleman than agriculture.

— Reading No. 9 —

RELIGION AND PHILOSOPHY

Formalism in Roman religion: comment published A.D. *77, but universally applicable; charm for an ailing ox [about 160* B.C.*]; Polybius on Roman religion as an opiate for the people [about 150* B.C.*]; Cicero on religion vs. superstition [44* B.C.*]; Augustus' deification [*A.D. *14]. Epicureanism praised by its greatest poet [about 55* B.C.*], and an Epicurean vilified by Rome's greatest orator [55* B.C.*]; Stoic ethics pompously summarized [about* A.D. *63]. Finally, a Stoic emperor warns himself against pomposity [about* A.D. *174].*

✓ ✓ ✓

a. PLINY: *Natural History*, XXVIII, 10-12

Sacrificing animals without prayer apparently does not work, nor produce the right ritual relation with the gods. Formulas vary; one to get good omens, another to avert bad ones, a third to praise the gods. . . . The chief magistrates pray by fixed formulae, taking precautions not to omit or misplace words; one person reads the prayer from a written text, the magistrate repeating it phrase by phrase; another checks it meticulously as recited; a third commands holy silence; a flutist drowns out ill-omened noises. They carefully tabulate occasions when sinister sounds or floundering have spoiled prayers. . . . Even in our own day a male and a female Greek, or victims from other hostile nations, have been buried alive in the Cattle Market. To peruse the prayer used in this ritual is to admit the efficacy of the formulas, all tested by the experience of 830 years.

b. CATO THE ELDER: *On Agriculture,* 83

Make the offering for the health of your oxen thus,
annually, if you wish: to Mars Silvanus, in the forest, in
daylight, one offering for each ox, by slave or freeman:
3 pounds whole wheat, 4½ pounds lard, 4½ pounds
meat, in one vessel; 3 pints wine in another. After the
ceremony, eat the offering on the spot. Women may not
attend this ceremony or see how it is performed.

---

c. POLYBIUS: *Histories,* VI, 56, 6-12

The Roman constitution's greatest superiority lies, I
think, in its attitude toward religion; indeed superstition,
which other peoples condemn, is what holds the Roman
state together. Religion's pomp, and its intimate involvement with public and private life are extraordinary and
will appear surprising. They have introduced it, I think,
for the sake of the common people. If a state consisting
of intellectuals had been feasible, this course would perhaps not have been necessary, but as the mob is invariably unstable, full of mutinous desires, irrational anger,
and violent passion, the only recourse is to restrain it
by invisible bugbears, pomp, and circumstance. Therefore
the ancients, I hold, did not act rashly and at random in
inculcating into the people ideas about the gods and convictions about Hell; rather, it is the moderns who are rash
and unintelligent to discard them.

---

d. CICERO: *On Divination,* II, 148-149

I want it clearly understood that I do not want religion
destroyed along with superstition. For it is the wise man's
business to protect ancestral institutions by retaining the
old rites and ceremonies. That some eternal supreme
Being exists, and that the human race ought to revere and
admire Him, is an admission to which the beauty of the
universe and the orderliness of the celestial bodies compel us. Therefore, just as religion, being associated with
natural science, ought actually to be propagated, so every
root of superstition ought to be weeded out. For it looms

over you, presses hard upon you, and pursues you wherever you turn, whether you listen to a hedge-priest or to
the interpretation of an omen, whether you make a sacrifice or watch the flight of a bird, or visit an astrologer
or a soothsayer, or if there is lightning or thunder, or a
bolt from the blue, or some monstrous birth or prodigious
occurrence.

---

e. DIO CASSIUS: *Roman History*, LVI, 46

They [the Senate] proclaimed Augustus immortal, and
decreed him priests and a ritual, with Livia . . . as his
priestess, and a lictor assigned her for use in discharging
her religious duties. Livia presented a million sesterces to
one Numerius Atticus, for swearing he had seen Augustus
ascending into Heaven, like . . . Romulus. The Senate
voted, and Livia and Tiberius built, a shrine to Augustus
in Rome, and others were built by communities elsewhere,
some voluntarily, some not. Also the house in Nola where
he died was set apart as a sanctuary. While his shrine in
Rome was building, they put a golden image of him on
a bed in the temple of Mars, and worshiped it exactly as
later they were to worship his statue. These miscellaneous
honors were voted him: his likeness should not be carried
in anyone's funeral cortège; the consuls should observe
his birthday with games, the Augustalia; the tribunes,
being sacrosanct, should direct them. . . . In addition,
Livia honored him with three days of private ceremonies
on the Palatine, an observance still continued by present
Emperors.

---

f. LUCRETIUS: *On the Nature of Things,* III, 1-6, 14-22, 28-40 (tr. A. D. Winspear, 1952)*

Into thick darkness came of old bright light.
You do I follow, you, who brought the light
To show us what is good and bad in life,
You do I follow, glory of the Grecian race,

* Reprinted, with permission of the copyright owners, the
  Regents of the University of Wisconsin, from *The Clas-
  sics in Translation,* Volume II, 1952, The University of
  Wisconsin Press.

And in your footsteps firmly plant my own.
Not that I want to rival you; affection makes me want to
    imitate. . . .
Soon as your thought, born of a godlike mind,
Begins to thunder forth on Nature's laws,
Then all terrors from our spirits flee;
The ramparts of the world are torn apart.
I see the atoms' pageant streaming through the void.
The power of godhead is revealed,
The quiet untroubled haunts of deity,
Which are not shaken by the wanton winds,
Nor lashed from cloud with rain.
No snow falls white nor frost assails;
Cloudless the air that covers them, and heaven bounte-
    ously smiles,
And sky is bathed in light. . . .
And so, thinking your thoughts
And with your guidance mastering science
A kind of godlike pleasure comes on me,
Pleasure and horror mixed,
Because your power of mind has left the works of nature
    naked to my view.

    Now since I have discoursed on atoms and have shown
What kind they are, how different in shape,
And how, self-moved, they ever fly,
In motion everlasting e'er impelled,
And how from atoms every object can be made,
Now I must tear up by the roots and cast away
That fear of death,
That fear that sullies mortal life from end to end
And pours the murk of death on everything,
Leaves no man's pleasure pure and unalloyed.

----

g. CICERO: *Against Piso,* passim

[*Epithets applied to an Epicurean:*] Fiend, filth, scoun-
drel, cook-shop consul, brute, lump of carrion, abandoned
carcass, gelded hog, Epicurean outlander, filthy boozer,
dog, foul and inhuman monster; degraded, half-dead
creature; pig from Epicurus' sty, thief, temple-robber,
assassin, vulture, blot, mannikin, Epicurus of mud and

clay, darkness personified, smut, bemired and dingy soul;
shattered, groveling, degraded, mean grandson of an auc-
tioneer; craven coward, scourge, destructive demon. . . .

---

h. SENECA: *Natural Questions,* III, *Preface,* 11-17

What is the paramount thing? To elevate your mind
above fortune's threats and promises, to consider all your
hopes as worthless. For what desirable thing can fortune offer? . . .

What is the paramount thing? To be able to bear adversity lightheartedly; to endure whatever happens as if
you wanted it that way (as you should, if you had known
that everything happens by divine decree). Weeping,
complaining, groaning—these are mutiny.

What is the paramount thing? A mind brave and de-
fiant in the teeth of disaster, not merely at odds, but at
daggers drawn, with luxury; neither open-armed nor a
runaway in the face of danger; knowing how to shape
your fortune instead of waiting for it; facing bad luck or
good untrembling and unconfused, unimpressed by the
turmoil of the one or the glitter of the other.

What is the paramount thing? Not to admit into the
mind evil communications, to raise clean hands to
Heaven, to pursue no benefit whose coming to you involves someone else's sacrifice or loss, to pray for what
no one will begrudge you: a pure heart; to regard all
else that mortals value, even though chance bring it to
your door, as fated to leave the way it came.

What is the paramount thing? To be ready to slip life's
moorings. This makes you free, not by the Roman's law
but by Nature's. He is truly free who has escaped from
self-enslavement, which is unrelenting, ineluctable, an
equal incubus by day and night, unceasing, unintermit-
tent. Self-enslavement is a millstone: you can shake it
off, if you will stop driving yourself, stop expecting rec-
ompense; if you will keep ever in mind your nature and
your age, however young, and say to yourself: "Why do
I rave, pant, sweat? Why do I walk my rut in town or
country? My needs are little, and they are not for long."

i. MARCUS AURELIUS: *Meditations*, IX, 29

How cheap are the mannikins who play the civic leader, like philosophers, in their own conceit! This is all folly! What then, O man? Do nature's bidding. Live strenuously, if you are cast in that role, and do not look about to see if anyone is noticing. Do not hope for Utopias, but be satisfied with the slightest progress, and count the upshot of your activity as of little worth. For who can change another's heart? Yet without a change of heart you have nothing but the slavery of men pretending to be persuaded, but really resentful. You will bring up Alexander, Philip, Demetrius of Phalerum. Whether they knew nature's will and trained themselves to follow it is their business. But if they played the Tragic King, no one has sentenced me to imitate them. Philosophy's function is a simple and humble one; lead me not astray into pomposity and putting on airs.

THE ROMANS AND THE LAND

Plutarch on Cato as a capital farmer [dramatic date, about 160 B.C.]; Cato's advice on buying a farm [same date]; Appian on land grants for Octavian's veterans [dramatic date, 43 B.C.]; Varro on the decline of agriculture [37 B.C.]; Vergil on the loveliness of Italy and the joys of country life [30 B.C.]; Columella's verses on spring picnics and flowers [about A.D. 60]; Pliny the Elder on ranches ruining Italy [about A.D. 77]; and Tertullian on the civilizing effect of Roman agriculture [about A.D. 210].

↗   ↗   ↗

a. PLUTARCH: *Life of Cato the Elder*, xxi, 5

As he began to pay more attention to large income, he treated dirt-farming more as a pastime than as a source of profit, and made solid, safe capital investments: in ponds, hot springs, lands with fuller's earth, pitch works, wild pasture, woodlands, from all of which he derived a large income and could not, he used to say, be ruined by a bad season.

————

b. CATO THE ELDER: *On Agriculture*, Preface, and I

One can sometimes make more money in trade, but it is so risky, or in money-lending, too, but it is so demeaning. When our ancestors . . . wanted to pay a good man a high compliment, they called him "good farmer," "good ploughman." . . . Farmers make the bravest heroes, the sturdiest soldiers, and . . . the least subversive citizens. . . .

When you think of buying a farm . . . it should have a good climate . . . and fertile soil. If possible, it should lie at the foot of a mountain, facing south, in a healthy spot with a good labor supply. It should be well watered, near a good-sized town, the sea, a navigable river, or a good main road. It should be in an area where farms do not often change owners, and where those who sell regret it. See that the farm buildings are solidly built. . . . If you ask me what the best kind of farm is, I should say 100 *jugera* of varied soils in a good location. A vineyard comes first if the vintage is good and copious; second, an irrigated garden; third, a planting of willows; fourth, an olive grove; fifth, pasture; sixth, grain land; seventh, a woodlot; eighth, an orchard; ninth, a grove of oaks for acorns.

---

c. APPIAN: *Civil Wars,* V, 12-13

Assigning the veterans to colonies and alloting the land was a difficult business. The soldiers demanded the cities chosen for them before the war as prizes, whereas the cities demanded that all Italy should share the load, or should draw lots, and that the beneficiaries pay for the land, but there was no money. They kept coming to Rome, young and old, women and children, to Forum and temples, wailing and saying that they, good Italians, though they had done nothing wrong, were being driven from land and hearthside like prisoners of war. The Romans grieved and wept in sympathy, reflecting . . . that the colonies were being set up to crush democracy, that the triumvirs might have their mercenaries ready for emergencies. Octavian's explanation to the cities that the move was inevitable failed to satisfy them. The veterans trespassed arrogantly upon their neighbors, grabbing more than had been assigned them and choosing the best lands.

---

d. VARRO: *On Agriculture,* II, Preface, 3-4

Since nowadays nearly all family men have forsaken sickle and plough and slink into Rome, and would rather use their hands for applause in theater and circus than for toil in field and vineyard, we hire someone to import grain to feed us from Africa and Sardinia, and the wine we lay down comes by ship from the islands of Cos and Chios. And so in the land where the shepherds who founded the city taught their children how to farm, nowadays their greedy and perverse descendants illegally make pasture out of grain land.

———

e. VERGIL: *Georgics* II, 136-176; 458-474*
(tr. S. Palmer Bovie, 1956)

But not the groves of Media, wealthy land,
Nor lovely Ganges, nor the golden streams
Of Lydia match Italy in praise;
Not India, Afghanistan, nor isles
Of Araby with incense-bearing sands.
No fiery bulls ploughed Italy's black soil
To sow a crop of giant dragon's teeth,
No human warriors sprang full-armed from her fields:
But teeming fruit and wine of the Campagna
Filled our Italian fields; fat herds and olives
Found their place in Italy's rich land.
Hence, the charger prancing in the plain;
Hence, white sheep and sacrificial bull,
So often plunged in Umbria's sacred streams,
Precede our Roman triumphs to the temples.
Here Spring persists, and Summer makes her way
Through foreign months: the flocks bear twice a year,
And twice the useful tree yields up her apples;
No raving tigers, savage lion cubs:
No poison wolfsbane fools the poor herb-gatherers.
No scaly reptile hustles huge coils across
The ground—or stops and winds his train in spirals.
See our noble cities, labor's crown,
Built breathlessly upon steep mountainsides,
Deep rivers flowing under ancient walls!
Shall I name the seas on either side?
Our inland lakes—you, Larian Como, the greatest,

* Reprinted from *Georgics of Vergil,* translated by S. Palmer
    Bovie, by permission of the University of Chicago Press.

And you, oh Garda, whose sea-waves plunge and roar?
Recall the Julian Port at Lake Lucrine
Where the channeled Tyrrhene flows into Avernus,
And the jetties thrust against the indignant sea
With a hissing surge, where Julian water sings
Its distant tones of tidal solitude?
Our land is veined with silver, copper, gold.
Italian soil has bred a race of heroes,
Marsians, Sabines, toughened generations
From the Western Coast, and tribes of Volscians
Handy with the spear. Great family names,
Camillus, Decius, Marius, Scipio,
And, chief of all, Octavianus Caesar,
Who triumphs now on Asia's farthest shore,
And defends the hills of Rome from the timid foe.
All hail, Saturnian Land, our honored Mother!
For thee I broach these themes of ancient art
And dare disclose the sacred springs of verse,
Singing Hesiod's song through Roman towns. . . .

Oh that farmers understood their blessings!
Their boundless joys! A land far off from war
Pours forth her fruit abundantly for them.
Although no stately home with handsome portals
Disgorges on its step a wave of callers
Every morning, gaping at his doors
Inlaid with tortoise shell, astonished by
His gold-trimmed clothes and his Corinthian bronzes,
Although his white wool is not stained with dye,
His oil not spoiled with perfumes from the East,
His rest is sound, his life devoid of guile.
His gains are manifold, his holdings broad:
Caves and living lakes, refreshing vales,
The cattle lowing, slumber in the shade.
Familiar with the haunts of animals,
The farmer lives in peace, his children all
Learn how to work, respect frugality,
Venerate their fathers and the gods:
Surely, Justice, as she left the earth,
In parting left her final traces here.

f. COLUMELLA: *On Agriculture,* X, 255-262, 275-285

Now of a sudden the springtime with fragrance of flow'rs
is upon us,

Now comes the time of the purple of spring, and the
fostering mother,

Earth, takes delight in decking her brows with blooms
many-colored.

Now the Phrygian trefoil opes its eyes like glistening
jewels,

Violets now from their slumbers unclose their fluttering
eyelids,

Snapdragons yawn in their beds, and roses with innocent
blushes

Mantle their virginal cheeks and piously mingle their
fragrance

Through all their shrines of the gods with the odor of
Arabic incense. . . .

Nymphs and Proserpine dear, lay aside your fears and
your mourning:

Turn unto us the light pit-a-pat of your delicate footsteps.

Take, holy ones, of the blossoms of earth, to the brim
of your baskets.

Here are no snares set for nymphs, no fear of a kidnap-
per's clutches.

Here holy Faith has her shrine, and the gods of the
household are worshiped.

Here there is nothing but fun, and carefree ripples of
laughter.

Drinking the first of the wine, we lunch on the grass and
are happy.

Now comes the mildness of spring, the softest and gen-
tlest of seasons:

Fresh and new is the sun, fresh and new the grass that we
lie on.

Now we may drink with delight from the brooklets that
run through the greensward,

Past is the nip of the frost, yet to come is the season of
sunstroke.

g. PLINY THE ELDER: *Natural History,* XVIII, 35

Medium-sized holdings of land were what the ancients believed in, thinking it better to sow less and plough more efficiently. . . . The fact is that large holdings have ruined Italy and before long will ruin the provinces too: six proprietors owned half the province of Africa when Nero had them killed.

---

h. TERTULLIAN: *On the Soul,* 30, 3

Flourishing farms have canceled out the desert, tilled fields have tamed the forests, flocks and herds have put wild beasts to flight. Sandy places are seeded, rocky places planted, marshes drained; as many cities now as shepherds' huts formerly. Desert islands are no longer fearsome; reefs have no terrors. Everywhere houses, people, law and order, civilized life.

— Reading No. 11 —

ROMAN LAW

*The introduction to Justinian's Institutes [A.D. 533];
passages from the account in* Acts *of Paul before the
Roman governor [about A.D. 60]; sections from the
charter [44 B.C.] of a Roman colony in Spain, to illustrate
fairness to defendants; Justinian's* Institutes, *on civil law,
natural law, and the law of nations; provisions from the
Twelve Tables [traditional date 449 B.C.], on posting
bond, against false witness, and assuring due process;
Cicero on the prestige of jurisprudents [55 B.C.]; the in-
stitution of the praetor for foreigners [dramatic date 242
B.C.]; more from Justinian's* Institutes *on the law of nations; Gaius [about A.D. 161] on mitigation of the lot
of slaves; passages from Gaius and Justinian to illustrate
the threefold division of Roman law into Persons, Things,
and Actions; and a rhetorical passage from the preface to
Justinian's* Institutes.

✓   ✓   ✓

a. JUSTINIAN: *Institutes,* I, i, 1, 3, and 4

Justice is the constant, unceasing desire to render to
each man his due. . . . The precepts of the Law are
these: to live honorably, not to injure another, to render
to each man his due. . . . Public law affects the constitution; private law concerns individual's interest. . . .
Private law has three parts; it is a collection of precepts
from natural law, the law of nations, and civil law.

———

b. *Acts of the Apostles:* xxii, 25-28; xxv, 10-12, 16

And as they bound him with thongs, Paul said unto

the centurion that stood by, Is it lawful for you to scourge
a man that is a Roman, and uncondemned? When the
centurion heard that, he went and told the chief captain,
saying, Take heed what thou doest, for this man is a
Roman. Then the chief captain came, and said unto him,
Tell me, art thou a Roman? He said, Yea. And the chief
captain answered, With a great sum obtained I this freedom. And Paul said, But I was free born. . . . [*Paul
is taken before the Roman governor, and says:*] I stand
at Caesar's judgment seat, where I ought to be judged: to
the Jews have I done no wrong, as thou very well knowest. For if I be an offender, or have committed anything
worthy of death, I refuse not to die: but if there by none
of these things whereof these accuse me, no man may
deliver me unto them. I appeal unto Caesar. Then Festus,
when he had conferred with the council, answered, Hast
thou appealed unto Caesar? Unto Caesar shalt thou go.
. . . [*Festus declares to the Jews the principle of Roman
law:*] It is not the manner of the Romans to deliver any
man to die, before that he which is accused have the
accusers face to face, and have license to answer for
himself concerning the crime laid against him.

c. *Law of the Colonia Genetiva Julia,* 102 (Bruns-
Gradenwitz, *Fontes Iuris Romani*[7], No. 28, pp. 133-134)

No chief magistrate, conducting an investigation or
trial under this law, shall, unless this law limits the
trial to one day, hold court before the first or after the
eleventh hour. As to the several accusers, the chief magistrate shall allow the chief accuser four hours, and each
subordinate accuser two, to make his case. . . . Whatever number of hours in all is granted to all the accusers
in each session, the chief magistrate shall grant to the
defendant or his spokesman twice as many.

d. JUSTINIAN: *Institutes,* I, 2, 1

Natural law is what nature has taught all living things.
. . . The difference between civil law and the law of nations is this: all peoples governed by laws and customs use
a legal system which is partly their own, partly shared

by all mankind. What a given people has established for itself as law is peculiar to that state, and is called civil law, . . . but what natural reason has established among all men is equally cherished among all peoples, and is called the law of nations. Therefore the Roman people uses partly its own particular civil law, partly the Law common to all mankind.

---

e. The XII Tables, II, 1; VIII, 23; IX, 1-3, 6, Bruns-Gradenwitz, *op. cit.*, pp. 20, 33, 34-35

When the object in dispute is worth 1,000 asses or more, each party shall deposit 500 asses; when less, fifty. When the object in dispute is the liberty of a slave, no matter how valuable, the deposit shall be fifty asses. [*Gaius,* Institutes, *IV, 14, adds:* This favors liberty, the purpose being not to let the magnitude of the risk deter the person asserting liberty.]

Whoever is convicted of giving false witness shall be thrown down from the Tarpeian Rock.

No one shall propose to deprive a person of civil rights without a civil trial; cases affecting civil rights shall not be decided except by the greatest assembly. . . .

Any legally constituted judge or arbitrator who is convicted of taking a bribe for a decision shall suffer the death penalty.

For any man whatsoever to be put to death without trial is forbidden.

---

f. CICERO: *On the Orator,* I, 198

Who does not know how much prestige, gratitude, and authority the study of the civil law brings to leading jurisconsults? Ours are not, as in Greece, mere low fellows, attracted by the smell of a fee, who offer themselves as assistants to pleaders. . . . Among us, on the contrary, the most distinguished and famous men have been jurisconsults. . . . Their ability first brought them eminence; in time their wise advice on the law brought

them influence based even more on reputation than on
ability.

---

g. JUSTINIAN: *Digest,* I, ii, 2, 27-28

Since the consuls were called away by wars against
their neighbors, leaving no one in the city to administer
justice, the office of urban praetor was created. Then
after some years, this praetor being inadequate because
of the host of foreigners who had migrated to the city,
another praetor was created, called the praetor for
foreigners, because his main duty was to settle cases
between foreigners.

---

h. JUSTINIAN: *Institutes,* I, 2, 2

The law of nations is common to the whole human
race. Prompted by experience and human needs, the races
of mankind have established certain rules for themselves.
For wars arose, and captivity and servitude followed,
which are contrary to natural law; for by natural law all
men were born free from the beginning. In accordance
with this law of nations almost all contracts have been introduced: purchase, sale, lease, hire, partnership, deposit,
loan, and innumerable others.

---

i. GAIUS: *Institutes,* I, 53

Nowadays neither Roman citizens nor any other person under Roman authority may be excessively or unrea-
sonably harsh to their slaves. By a ruling of the Emperor
Antoninus, whoever without cause kills his own slave is
held not less liable to punishment than a man who kills
someone else's slave. And excessive cruelty of masters
is restrained by a ruling of the same Emperor; in reply
to enquiries by heads of provinces about slaves who take
sanctuary at the temples of the gods or the statues of
emperors, he laid it down that if the cruelty of masters
seemed intolerable they should be forced to sell their
slaves.

j. GAIUS: *Institutes,* I, 29

[*Example of the Law of Persons.*] When a slave under thirty years of age is freed, acquires Latin rights, and marries a Roman citizen, a Latin colonist, or a freedwoman of the same condition as himself, and these facts are attested by not less than seven witnesses, Roman citizens above the age of puberty, and begets a son, when that son reaches the age of one year, the father is entitled to apply to the praetor, or, in the provinces, to the head of the province, and to prove that he has married a wife and by her has had a son now one year old. And if the person to whom the proof is submitted proclaim the truth of the facts, then that freedman of Latin rights, and his wife, if she is of the same condition, and the son, if he is of the same condition, are legally Roman citizens.

k. JUSTINIAN: *Institutes,* II, i, 39

[*Example of the Law of Things.*] As to treasure found by anyone on his own property, the deified Hadrian, following natural equity, granted it to the finder. The same applied to finding a treasure accidentally in public or private consecrated ground. But if anyone found treasure on another's property, not deliberately searching, but by accident, he granted one one-half to the owner of the property. And on the same principle, if anyone found treasure on the Emperor's property, he stipulated half to the finder, half to the Emperor. On the same principle, if anyone finds treasure on property belonging to a city or to the treasury, half belongs to him, half to the treasury or the city.

l. JUSTINIAN: *Institutes,* IV, 16, 1-2

[*Example of the Law of Actions.*] Those who established our rights have taken great pains to keep people from bringing suit too easily; and this is our intention also. The most efficient way to restrain the litigiousness of plaintiffs and defendants is sometimes by a fine, sometimes by the obligation of an oath, sometimes by fear of infamy. For example, a ruling of ours imposes an oath on all defendants, for a defendant is not allowed to state his case unless he first swears that his plea of not guilty is made under the impression that he has a good case. In some suits an action for double or triple damages is laid against defendants who plead not guilty. . . . The litigiousness of plaintiffs and of advocates for each side is also restrained by oath; . . . and irresponsible litigants are required to pay to their adversary damages and costs. Some suits, for theft, robbery with violence, injury, fraud, involve infamy for the defendants if they are found guilty or if they settle the case out of court.

---

m. JUSTINIAN: *Institutes,* Preface, 1-2

In the name of our Lord Jesus Christ. The Emperor Caesar Flavius Justinian, conqueror of the Alemanni, Goths, Franks, Germans, Antians, Alans, Vandals, Africans, pious, happy, glorious, triumphant, ever Augustus, to young men eager to know the law: Our Imperial Majesty must be armed with laws as well as famous in arms, that both in war and peace the ship of state may be rightly steered, and the Roman Emperor not only stand forth victorious in battles against his enemies, but also expel by due process of law the injustices of wrong-doers, and become as scrupulous in justice as he is triumphant over conquered foes. By unceasing vigilance and forethought, with God's help we have accomplished both. The barbarian nations sent under our yoke recognize our exertions in war; . . . all peoples, too, are now ruled by laws promulgated or compiled by us. Having clarified, arranged, and brought into agreement imperial rulings previously in disorder, we then extended our attention to the countless volumes of ancient jurisprudence; and, sailing as it were uncharted seas, have now by Heaven's favor completed a task that seemed hopeless.

— Reading No. 12 —

THE ROAD TO ABSOLUTISM

A passage from a Hellenistic theorist [third or second century B.C.] shows the intellectual pedigree of the notion of the Roman emperor as a benevolent despot made in God's own image; the oath taken to Augustus by the Paphlagonians [3 B.C.]; informers, trial for subversive activity, and book-burning under Tiberius [A.D. 15, 23, and 25]; compulsion to public service in Egypt [about A.D. 90]; rulings of Marcus Aurelius [A.D. 161-180] and Septimius Severus [A.D. 193-211] restricting freedom of association; confiscations by the tyrannical Maximinus [A.D. 235-238]; an assessment of Diocletian [A.D. 284-305], prejudiced by his persecution of the Christians; selections from Diocletian's price-fixing edict [A.D. 301]; and an account of Constantius' pompous visit to Rome [A.D. 357].

✔   ✔   ✔

a. ECPHANTUS: *On Monarchy*, Stobaeus, *Anthology*, IV, vii, 64

Physically the king is like the rest of us, being made of the same material, but he has been better fashioned by the Divine Craftsman, using Himself as model. The king, then, is created separate and unique, a copy of the higher king, always on familiar terms with his Maker, appearing to his subjects as it were in a royal light. . . . Because God rules well, so does the king, and his subjects are well ruled. I assume, then that the king on earth can in no way be less excellent than the king in heaven, but as the king is an extraneous, foreign thing, heaven-sent to mankind, so one would assume that his excellences are God's work and belong to him through God.

b. Oath of Gangra, Paphlagonia (Dessau, *I.L.S.* 8781)

I swear by Zeus, Earth, Sun, all gods and goddesses, and Augustus himself to be loyal to Caesar Augustus, his children, and his children's children all my life long in word, deed, and thought, considering to be friends those whom they so consider, and enemies those whom they so judge. In their interest I will spare neither body, soul, life, nor children, but in all ways will undergo all risks for their welfare. Whenever I notice or hear anything said, plotted, or done against them, I will become an informer about it, and will hold the sayer, plotter, or doer in enmity. And whomsoever they judge enemies, these on land and sea with weapons of steel I swear to pursue and ward off. If I do anything counter to this oath, . . . I imprecate upon myself, my body, soul, life, children and all my kith and kin forever complete ruin and annihilation. May neither earth nor sea receive the bodies of my family or my posterity; let the earth bear them no fruit.

---

c. TACITUS: *Annals,* I, 74; IV, 30 and 34-35 (abridged)

Caepio entered upon a way of life which, thanks to troubled times and human intolerance, soon became crowded. A penniless, obscure busybody, he first used his private files on subversion to worm his way into Tiberius' pitiless confidence, finally jeopardizing the whole aristocracy. From the monarch he got power, from everyone else, loathing. His imitators rose from poverty to riches, from inspiring scorn to inspiring terror; the ruin they contrived for others recoiled finally upon themselves.

The Senate was debating the abolition of rewards for informers in cases where a man accused of subversion committed suicide before the trial ended. As they were about to vote for it, Tiberius, rather irritably, and with a frankness quite unlike him, took the informers' part, growling that this would invalidate the statutes, undermine the constitution; better subvert the laws than take away their watchdogs. Thus the breed of informers, the curse of mankind, whom no penalties could muzzle, were actually encouraged with prizes.

———

The charge against Cremutius Cordus was novel and hitherto unheard-of: that of publishing a history praising Brutus and calling Cassius the last of the Romans. Cremutius, who had made up his mind to suicide, said in a speech, . . . "Livy . . . praised Pompey so highly that Augustus called him his Pompeian, but it did not affect their friendship. . . . To Cicero's book which made practically a god of Cato, Caesar the dictator made no more savage reply than a speech in rebuttal, as though before a jury. . . . Catullus' poetry, brimful of invective against the Caesars, is still read; the deified Julius and Augustus, equally admirable for tolerance and for common sense, put up with these works and left them alone. . . . For attacks ignored are forgotten; taking them seriously seems to lend them notoriety. . . . Posterity allots every man his share of fame; my doom may be immanent, but the world will remember me along with Brutus and Cassius." Then he left the Senate and starved himself to death. The aediles burned his books by Senate decree; but a hidden set survived, and they were republished, to make a laughing-stock of stupid men who think tyranny now can erase the record of history hereafter. No, to persecute genius is to exalt its prestige; foreign potentates, and imitators of their ruthlessness, have only bred obloquy for themselves and glorious martryrdom for their victims.

———

d. Pap. Vind. 25824b II-III: *Museum Helveticum,*
II (1945) 57-58

From Mettius Rufus' orders to the district governors. If any persons liable for compulsory public service seem to you unqualified either through inadequate income, physical unfitness, or any other reason, send me three nominations for each vacancy, after checking their qualifications not only as to income, but also as to age and a way of life appropriate to those entrusted with imperial business. Therefore, include in your report income, age, literacy, and public posts previously held. See that the three are not related, nor from the same household or district, that they have not held the same posts before, or been convicted of misconduct in previous positions.

e. JUSTINIAN: *Digest,* XLVII, 22, 1-2

Imperial rulings direct heads of provinces not to allow political associations, including those of soldiers in camp. But the lower classes are allowed to pay monthly dues, provided they meet only once a month, and no subversive association may meet under any such pretext. . . . Meeting for religious purposes is not forbidden, provided such meetings do not contravene the Senate's decree against subversive associations. No one may legally belong to more than one association. . . . Whosoever presumes to operate a subversive association is executed in the same way as traitors who occupy public places or temples with troops.

f. HERODIAN: *From the Death of the Deified Marcus,* VII, 3

What was the good of wiping out the barbarians, if the slaughter in Rome itself and among her subject peoples grew greater than ever? What was the good of carrying off spoils from the enemy, if one was to be despoiled oneself and see one's kinsmen's property confiscated? Informers were free, or rather positively encouraged, to do their dirty work, to scrape together at will unheard-of and therefore irrefutable scandals about one's ancestors. The mere summons to court by an informer was tantamount to conviction and confiscation of all property. Every day one could see yesterday's millionaires faced with a life of beggary, so greedy was [Maximinus'] despotism, under pretext of constant levies for military supplies. . . . He would order his victims, alone, and without a retinue, to be set in wagons and travel night and day from east, west and south to Paeonia, where he was, and he would strip and revile them and sentence them to exile or death.

These individual cases . . . did not matter much to the urban or provincial masses, who did not worry about the misfortunes of those assumed to be prosperous. Some spiteful, envious commoners are actually pleased to see the high and mighty ruined. But then Maximinus, having reduced most of the noble houses to penury, and finding the proceeds slight and inadequate for his wishes, began to appropriate public funds, whether earmarked for dole or donative, for the theatre or for religious festivals. Dedications in temples, statues of gods, tributes to heroes, whatever public adornment a city had that could be made into coin, he melted it all down. . . . Then indeed in the cities and provinces the masses fumed in their very souls. Holding the soldiers responsible for the extortions, relatives and friends reviled them hatefully, believing that Maximinus was doing this for the soldiers' sake.

g. LACTANTIUS: *On the Deaths of the Persecutors,* vii

Diocletian, deviser of crimes and designer of evils, ruined everything, not withholding his hands from God Himself. His greed and his cowardice turned the whole world upside down. For he shared his empire with three others, dividing the world into four parts and multiplying armies, each ruler competing to have a far larger force than former emperors had had when they ruled the state alone. The number of recipients of public funds began to be so much greater than the number of taxpayers that the colossal assessments ruined the tenant farmers, fields were deserted, and tilled acres reverted to wasteland. To make terror universal, the provinces also were sliced up; swarms of governors and minor officers battened upon each region and almost on each city; likewise treasury agents, bureaucrats, and prefects' deputies, before all of whom due process was quite rare, but convictions and confiscations numerous, manifold extortions not merely frequent but constant, and practiced with intolerable injustice. . . . When by various unfair practices he had caused incalculable inflation, he tried to fix commodity prices by law. This caused much bloodshed over petty trifles, fear kept everything off the market, and prices grew still worse inflated, until from sheer necessity, after much loss of life, the law was repealed.

---

h. DIOCLETIAN: *Price Edict* (H. Blümner, *Der Maximaltarif des Diocletian* [Berlin, 1893], pp. 7-50, selections)

We therefore take the initiative in prescribing remedies for a chronic problem, knowing that no complaints that our intervention is untimely, superfluous, unimportant, or trifling can justly come from profiteers who have seen in our long silence a lesson in self-control which they have been unwilling to follow. For who can be so obtuse and inhuman as to be unaware that in sales in the market and in daily transactions in the cities runaway inflation is so widespread that neither plentiful supplies nor bountiful harvests relieve unbridled lust for profit? . . . We have therefore decided that maximum prices must be fixed for articles for sale. . . . If anyone dares to contravene the letter of this statute, he shall be subject to capital punishment. . . . The maximum allowable prices for the sale of individual items are set forth below [*selections from a much longer list*]:

Wheat, per army peck	100	denarii
Wine, ordinary, per Italian pint	8	"
Beer, Egyptian, per Italian pint	2	"
Oil, B-grade, per Italian pint	24	"
Beef, per Italian pound	8	"
Salt fish, per Italian pound	6	"
Farm laborer's wages, with found, per day	25	"
Picture painter's wages, with found, per day	150	"
Shepherd's wages, with found, per day	20	"
Elementary teacher's wages, per pupil per month	50	"
Professor of rhetoric's wages, per pupil per month	250	"
Advocate or jurist, fee for pleading	1,000	"
Soldier's boots, without hobnails	100	"
Freight, ass load, per mile	4	"
Raw silk, dyed purple, per pound	150,000	"

i. AMMIANUS MARCELLINUS: *History*, XVI, 10

Constantius . . . hankered to see Rome, . . . to celebrate a triumph over Roman blood, though he had never personally conquered any hostile nation . . . nor added anything to the Empire. . . . But he wanted to display a very long parade, banners stiff with gold, and a handsome retinue before a peace-loving populace who neither expected nor wanted any such thing. . . . So, puffed up with great honors, escorted by fearsome troops, he was conducted [to the city] in battle array, the cynosure of all eyes. . . . He sat alone in a golden chariot, gleaming with the brightness of assorted jewels, whose sparkle rivalled the sunlight. . . . Though he was very short, he stooped when passing under lofty gates, and, as if his neck were clamped in a vise, he kept his eyes straight ahead, and turned his face neither left nor right, as though he were a dummy; he was never seen to bob up and down with the jolting of the wheels, or spit, or wipe or stroke his face or nose, or gesticulate. . . . During his whole reign he never invited anyone to sit beside him in a vehicle, nor took any private citizen as colleague in the consulship, as other consecrated emperors had, and, puffed up with his own lofty self-importance, he had many other similar habits which he observed as rigorously as if they were the justest of laws.

— Reading No. 13 —

ROME AND CHRISTIANITY

Nero persecutes the Christians for allegedly setting Rome's great fire of A.D. 64; Pliny as governor of Bithynia [about A.D. 112] asks Trajan how trials of Christians should be conducted; the Emperor's reply bids him ignore anonymous accusations. Justin Martyr [about A.D. 150] tells how early Christians kept Sunday; a passage from the Apocryphal New Testament [about A.D. 150] presents St. John the Evangelist drawing a moral from bedbugs; Senate minutes [A.D. 176] hail condemned Christians as a cheap source of material for gladiatorial shows; Cyprian describes Valerian's persecutions [A.D. 257]; the so-called "Edict of Milan" [A.D. 313] grants Christians and pagans freedom of worship; finally, two rulings [A.D. 313 and 326] exempt priests from compulsory public service but exclude heretics from privileges granted to Catholic Christians.

✓ ✓ ✓

a. TACITUS: *Annals,* XV, 44

But no human ingenuity, no imperial hush-money or fawning upon the gods could rid Nero of suspicion of having ordered the fire set. So, to spike the rumors, he supplied scapegoats, inflicting the most far-fetched tortures upon the so-called Christians, whom the mob hated for their scandalous conduct. They are named after their founder, Christ, who was crucified under Tiberius by the procurator Pontius Pilate. This momentarily halted this dangerous fanaticism, but it broke out anew, not only in Judea, where this evil originated, but also in Rome, concentration and dissemination point for everything malevolent and shameful from all over the world. Those first arrested confessed; then their evidence convicted others in droves, not so much of arson as of hatred of mankind. Their executions became sports events: they were covered with wild animal skins and torn apart by dogs, or crucified and set on fire to supply light at night. . . . Therefore, though they were malefactors deserving the severest punishments, sympathy arose, since they were being executed not in the public interest, but to satisfy a sadistic tyrant.

---

b. PLINY THE YOUNGER: *Letters,* X, 96 and 97 (abridged)

Pliny to Trajan: My procedure in cases involving alleged Christians has been this: I asked them if they were Christians. If they admitted it, I asked them a second and a third time, threatening punishment. If they continued recalcitrant, I ordered them executed, convinced that whatever the nature of their faith, their obduracy and unyielding stubbornness deserved punishment. Other similar fanatics, being Roman citizens, I put down for transport to Rome. Soon the trials produced, as usual, new and varied charges. A long list of names was posted anonymously. Those who denied that they were or had been Christians, and following after me, prayed to the gods, offered incense and wine to your statute . . . and cursed Christ (which no real Christian, they say, will ever do) I thought should be let go. Others, named by an informer, first said they were Christians and then denied it; some claimed to have given it up as many as twenty years ago. All these, too, worshiped your image and the god's statues, and cursed Christ.

They claimed, moreover, that all their guilt or error amounted to was meeting at regular intervals, singing a hymn antiphonally to Christ as to a god, and swearing, without criminal intent, an oath to commit neither theft, brigandage, adultery, false witness, nor breach of trust. Then they would disband, and meet again to take an ordinary, harmless meal. They had stopped this practice after my edict, issued on your instructions, forbidding secret societies. So I thought it the more necessary to torture the truth out of two maidservants, called deaconesses, but all I discovered was a misguided fanaticism. . . .

I thought the matter worth consulting you about, especially as so many are and will be involved, of all ages and classes, and even of both sexes. This superstition has infected villages and farms as well as cities, but it can, I think, be restrained and remedied. At least there is this clear evidence: temples, formerly almost empty, begin to be thronged again, regular rituals, long in abeyance, to be celebrated; and sacrificial victims, until recently a drug on the market, are finding wide sale. This makes it easy to imagine how many people might be saved from error if offered a chance to repent.

Trajan to Pliny: You have followed proper procedure, my dear Pliny, in investigating cases of alleged Christians. No fixed, all-purpose rule can be laid down. You should not go looking for them; if they are reported and convicted, they must be punished; but anyone, however suspect in the past, who denies that he is a Christian, and proves he is not by worshiping our gods should be pardoned if he repents. To recognize anonymous accusations as evidence would set a thoroughly bad precedent and be contrary to the enlightened spirit of our age.

---

c. JUSTIN MARTYR: *First Apology,* lxvii

On the day called Sunday everyone gathers from city and country to hear brief readings from the acts of the apostles or the writings of the prophets. Then the person in charge, in a sermon, exhorts and invites us to follow their sterling example. Then we all rise together and pray, after which bread, wine, and water are brought, and the person in charge prays fervently and gives hearty thanks, while the people cry piously, "Amen!" Then the things for which thanks have been given are distributed and received, and the deacons send some to those absent. The well-to-do make voluntary contributions of any amount they like, and the collection is deposited with the person in charge. He supports widows, orphans, those left destitute by illness or any other affliction; prisoners, and strangers staying with us; in brief, he cares for all who are in need.

———

d. APOCRYPHAL NEW TESTAMENT: *Acts of John,* lx-lxi (tr. M. R. James, Oxford, 1924)*

Now on the first day we arrived at a deserted inn, and when we were at a loss for a bed for John, we saw a droll matter. There was one bedstead lying somewhere there without coverings, whereon we spread the cloaks which we were wearing, and we prayed him to lie down upon it and rest, while the rest of us all slept upon the floor. But he when he lay down was troubled by the bugs, and as they continued to become yet more troublesome to him, when it was now about the middle of the night, in the hearing of us all he said to them: I say unto you, O bugs, behave yourselves, one and all, and leave your abode for this night and remain quiet in one place, and keep your distance from the servants of God. And as we laughed, and went on talking for some time, John addressed himself to sleep; and we, thanks to him, were not disturbed.

But when the day was now dawning I arose first, and with me Verus and Andronicus, and we saw at the door of the house which we had taken a great number of bugs standing, and while we wondered at the great sight of them, and all the brethren were roused up because of them, John continued sleeping. And when he was awaked we declared to him what we had seen. And he sat up on the bed and looked at them and said: Since ye have well behaved yourselves in hearkening to my rebuke, come unto your place. And when he had said this, and risen from the bed, the bugs running from the door hasted to the bed and climbed up by the legs thereof and disappeared into the joints. And John said again: This creature hearkened unto the voice of a man, and abode by itself

———

* Reprinted by permission from *The Apocryphal New Testament* by Montague R. James, Clarendon Press, Oxford, 1924.

and was quiet and trespassed not; but we which hear the voice and commandments of God disobey and are light-minded: and for how long?

---

e. Roman Senate Minutes: J. H. Oliver, *Hesperia,* XXIV, p. 333, lines 29-35, 55-58 (adapted)

The maximum price for first-class gladiators shall be 5,000 to 15,000 sesterces; for second class 4,000-7,000; for third class 3,000-6,000, depending on the total expenses of a given spectacle. . . . But in the cities of the most noble Gallic provinces, of sacrificial victims, who because of traditional sacred ritual are eagerly awaited, let the trainers make delivery for no more than 2,000 sesterces apiece, since our mighty emperors have announced that their procurator will supply the trainers with condemned criminals at not more than six gold pieces each.

---

f. CYPRIAN: *Letters,* lxxx

I did not write to you at once, dearest brother, because all the clergy, taxed by the trials before them, must stay here [in Carthage] and hold themselves ready with dedicated hearts for the heavenly crown. Now the messengers I sent to Rome to find out the truth about the decree against us have come back. Many uncertain and contradictory rumors are circulating, but the truth is that Valerian in a memorandum to the Senate has demanded immediate execution for bishops, priests, and deacons. Senators, persons of quality, and Roman knights are to lose both rank and property. If they still continue to call themselves Christians, they are to be put to death. Matrons are to suffer confiscation of property and exile. Imperial finance officers who have been or are Christians are to suffer confiscation, be cast into chains, and assigned [as slaves] to the imperial domains. The Emperor appended a copy of a letter about us addressed to provincial governors. Daily expecting this letter's arrival, we stand firm in our faith and ready to suffer, awaiting from the Lord's merciful help the crown of eternal life. Sixtus

[Bishop of Rome] was executed in the cemetery August 6, and four deacons with him. The prefects at Rome press this persecution harder every day, executing all who come before them and confiscating their property. Please let our other colleagues know this news, so that everywhere their exhortations may comfort our brethren and prepare them for the spiritual struggle, so that each may think less about death than about immortality, and that, consecrated to the Lord with all the strength of their faith and courage, they may know joy rather than fear when they make the confession whereby they know that God's and Christ's soldiers suffer not death but coronation. I bid you, dearest brother, ever farewell.

---

g. EUSEBIUS: *Ecclesiastical History,* X, v, 5-6, 9-10
(much abridged)

I, Constantine Augustus, and I, Licinius Augustus, have resolved that absolutely no one be denied the right to follow and choose the Christian, or any other, form of worship, so that the Divinity may in all things grant us his usual kindly favor. The unfortunate stipulations, wholly at variance with our clemency, contained in our previous letters to your office about the Christians, are hereby cancelled. And now let every man desiring the Christian, or any other, form of worship be allowed to observe it freely and simply, without any hindrance. Moreover, with special reference to Christians, we decree that their former places of assembly, purchased from our treasury or elsewhere, or received by gift, shall be restored to the Christians without demand for cash payment or compensation, scrupulously and without double-dealing. If the purchasers or receivers by gift of such property desire anything of our generosity, let them apply to the district prefect.

---

h. EUSEBIUS: *Ecclesiastical History,* X, vii

I decree that all Catholic clerics under Caecilian's see in your province, who devote themselves to this holy worship, shall once and for all be kept free from compulsory public services, that they may not through any mistake or impious error be dragged away from the worship due the Divinity, but rather without any hindrance serve their own law. For in rendering supreme service to the Deity, I think they make the greatest possible contribution to the common weal.

---

i. *Theodosian Code,* XVI, v, 1

Privileges granted for religious considerations shall apply only to practitioners of the Catholic faith. We decree that heretics and schismatics not only be barred from these privileges, but be bound and subjected to the various compulsory public services.

A SHORT BIBLIOGRAPHY

General. The indispensable source book for documents in translation is N. Lewis and M. Reinhold, *Roman Civilization,* 2 vols. (New York: Columbia University Press, 1951-1955). Most Latin and Greek authors are translated in the Loeb Classical Library (Cambridge, Mass.: Harvard University Press). More and more are appearing in inexpensive paper-bound translations; for a recent list see *Classical Weekly* (now *Classical World*) LI (1958) 100-110. A standard reference work is the *Oxford Classical Dictionary* (Oxford University Press, 1949). A briefer handbook is Sir Paul Harvey, *Oxford Companion to Classical Literature* (*ib.,* 1937). *The Legacy of Rome,* ed. Cyril Bailey (*ib.,* 1923) contains essays on many of the topics discussed in this book. Roman *Realien* are described and well illustrated in M. Johnston, *Roman Life* (Chicago: Scott, Foresman, 1957). The standard histories are the *Cambridge Ancient History,* VII-XII (Cambridge University Press, 1928-1939) and Methuen's (London) *History of the Roman World: 753-146* B.C. (H. H. Scullard, 1951); *146-30* B.C. (F. B. Marsh, 1951); *30* B.C.-A.D. *138* (E. T. Salmon, 1950); A.D. *138-337* (H. M. D. Parker, 1935). For a recent treatment of Roman history see V. M. Scramuzza and P. MacKendrick, *The Ancient World,* chs. 32-59 (New York: Holt, 1958).

INDEX

184